July 21, 2008
Williams

SAMUEL CARTER

SAM

Our Church
A Holiness Heritage
in the Caribbean

by
Rev. Dr. Carlyle Williams

Foreword by
Rev. Dr. Carlston Christie

authorHOUSE®

AuthorHouse™
1663 Liberty Drive, Suite 200
Bloomington, IN 47403
www.authorhouse.com
Phone: 1-800-839-8640

© 2008 Rev. Dr. Carlyle Williams. All rights reserved.

No part of this book may be reproduced, stored in a retrieval system, or transmitted by any means without the written permission of the author.

First published by AuthorHouse   2/18/2008

ISBN: 978-1-4343-6074-8 (sc)

Library of Congress Control Number: 2008900533

Printed in the United States of America
Bloomington, Indiana

This book is printed on acid-free paper.

Table of Contents

FOREWORD vii

ACKNOWLEDGEMENTS ix

INTRODUCTION xi

CHAPTER I.
Holiness: Our Tradition Defined 1

CHAPTER II.
Holiness: The Nature of Our Divine God 9

CHAPTER III.
Holiness: The Lordship and Leadership of the Holy Spirit 13

CHAPTER IV.
Holiness: The Manner of the Experience 27

CHAPTER V.
Holiness: Our Tradition Became Our Holiness Heritage 31

CHAPTER VI.
Holiness: The Proclamation of Our Holiness Heritage Through Systematic Teaching 51

CHAPTER VII.
Holiness: The Development of Models for the Effective Communication of Holiness and Lifestyle Change for the Barbados Wesleyan Community 65

BIBLIOGRAPHY 97

TESTIMONIALS 101

FOREWORD

Wesleyan Church leaders have, from time to time, been accused of not committing to permanent record insights gleaned from their privileged positions of leadership and learning. A sister denomination is credited with having leaders who have written many books for the benefit of current and future disciples.

In writing *Repositioning Our Church through Our Holiness Heritage,* the Reverend Dr. Carlyle Williams has joined the ranks of those who have sought to nudge the Church forward through informed writing. He writes specifically for the benefit of the Wesleyan Holiness Church in Barbados. But what he has cited in respect to Barbados is applicable— if perhaps in varying measure —to the other districts of The Wesleyan Holiness Church in the Caribbean.

The book would also hold some interest for the many missionaries and indigenous leaders and their families whose labours of dedicated love have been honorably referred to within its pages. The author judges the missionary-led church to have been influential and successful in a measure that is no longer the case. He attributes this influence and success to a large extent to the ministry of the holiness movement and to the consequent lifestyle of its adherents. He sees "the age of technology, the age of tolerance, and the freedom of cross cultural church bonding" to be mainly responsible for the decline in stature of The Wesleyan Holiness Church in Barbados.

In calling for the denomination to develop "models for the effective communication of holiness" and for consequential lifestyle change, the author offers extensive curricular materials intended to assist in the realization of these models. His ultimate goal is the evangelization of Barbados communities through the dynamic ministry of The Wesleyan Holiness Church.

The Reverend Dr. Carlyle Williams has come up through the ranks of the Wesleyan Holiness Church in Barbados and has risen to the position of district superintendent, an office which he has held for the past twenty years. He writes, therefore, from a uniquely advantageous position. His call, then, for a revival in the preaching and practice of scriptural holiness, is one that deserves to be heard.

Rev. Dr. Carlston E. Christie
General Superintendent, Caribbean Wesleyan Holiness Church

ACKNOWLEDGEMENTS

The Wesleyan Holiness Church in Barbados has a great heritage of Holiness developed and transmitted through the past nine decades by great stalwarts of the Word of God and faith in Jesus Christ. When the truth of heart holiness is taught by able leaders, our society experiences a change which only the Holy Spirit can bring. Highest praise must be given to our Holy Father whose will and purpose is that all men be holy in this life time.

Thanks to our church parents for their commitment to the promotion of sound biblical truth and holy living which resulted in our birth into the Kingdom of God.

I must acknowledge all those persons who challenged and encouraged me in this research. Dr. Shelton Wood, Jr., my professor, who gave himself to the development and execution of this training programme in Barbados. He further encouraged me to pursue this wonderful programme, and indeed I am extremely grateful to him.

To Mrs. Beverley Lashley, my supervisor, Pastor Sylvan Puckerin and Rev Elsie Weir, who made it their duty to ensure that I was making the desired progress, I say thanks.

I hereby acknowledge the vital contributions by Mrs. Daphne Millington, whose historical data of the church, her biblical insights into our holiness heritage, as well as her use of English skills have made significant difference to my thesis.

To the many pastors and church members who gave of their time in the interviews and the completion of questionnaires, I say thank you.

Thanks to Mrs. Kathryn Bradshaw, my daughter, who has done a wonderful job in the arranging and producing of the finished document.

Thanks to my wife, Marguarette, for her support in every possible way as I pursued this challenging task. To God be the glory in making my ambition possible.

Rev. Carlyle Williams

INTRODUCTION

"The lines are fallen unto me in pleasant places; yea, I have a goodly heritage." Psalm 16:6

A heritage may be considered as that significant linkage of culture, ways or morés passed on from a progressing and existing family to an emerging one. The word 'heritage' is derived from the Latin "*heres* meaning 'heir' or what is or may be handed on to an individual from his ancestors, becoming a great cultural heritage from the circumstances of his birth."[1]

The Wesleyan Holiness Church, formerly the Pilgrim Holiness Church, has been endowed with a rich spiritual legacy which can be described as a holiness heritage. This fact has motivated the topic of this study.

Our Church fathers made a substantial investment in our Christian experience which, if it were to be fully embraced by us for our development, shared within our circle of influence and even beyond, would considerably change the character of our national landscape today. What a society would result! The trustworthiness, the mutual respect, the brotherly love and kindness, the productivity of our citizens and the powerful witness of the Holy Spirit within them would transform what is now a spiritually sick nation.

This study is designed to examine the quality of life which was transmitted and accepted by our Wesleyan Church fathers here

---

[1] Clarence L. Barnhart, The World Book Dictionary, (J.G. Ferguson Publishing Company., Chicago, U.S.A. 1983), p.992

in Barbados through the sacrificial ministry of overseas holiness kingdom builders as early as the year nineteen hundred and twelve (1912) in the city of Bridgetown, Barbados, although other evangelical churches had been at work since 1765. The message of heart purity and the lordship of the Holy Spirit, transformed a dark, sinful city into a nation of hardworking, honest and dignified people; it transformed grandsons and granddaughters of slaves into preachers and church leaders of holiness churches by the year nineteen hundred and thirty (1930). The fire of the Holy Spirit created the passion which transformed hopeless fathers and families from a pagan past to what was hoped would be an industrious, fruitful and honourable future church community.

The Holiness Church invested heavily in the development of children and youth within the first twenty (20) years of carrying out the kingdom principle as enunciated in Deuteronomy: "And thou shalt teach them diligently unto thy children, and shalt talk of them when thou sittest in thine house, and when thou walkest by the way, and when thou liest down, and when thou riseth up ... thou shalt fear the Lord thy God, and serve Him, and shalt swear by His name."
(Deut. 6:7, 13)

There was an urgency in the proclamation of the holiness message. There were already Pentecostal churches and other evangelical denominations in those early years of our church development, but the holiness heritage exemplified the holiness church. The Pilgrim Holiness Church members gained great notoriety for their strict and fiery preachers and pastors as well as for the holiness standards exemplified by their members. Even though one can admit to some simplistic extremes in the understanding of the externals, one must concede the obvious commitment to their love for God and the practice of the proclamation of heart holiness which resulted in rapid church growth: holiness or hell was the key concept.

There seemed to be a violent aversion to the spirit of the world by the holiness fathers from their early beginning at the Outlet Hall in the heart of Bridgetown in 1912, when corporate worship was held on the upper floor of a rum shop. The general feeling was, while the alcoholic spirits were distributed downstairs, the Holy Spirit was pouring out upstairs, as the saints touched heaven for earth below. Fire and outreach characterized that holiness beginning. The island of Barbados became their village as no distance was too great for them to undertake in order to share the wonderful news of lifestyle holiness.

It would seem today that we have outgrown that early holiness fire. This study is intended to define as clearly as possible that fire: its source, its purpose and power for all times. Can we really see and experience a resurgence of our holiness heritage? If Christian education and sanctification can bring behavioural change in any nation, then through this study it is hoped to provide some power, principles and programmes for behavioural change as the way forward for our Barbadian Wesleyan Holiness Church. There is dire need of a return to the systematic communication of the holiness message. Yes, we do have a goodly heritage; but we need to pass it on intelligently and in the power of the Holy Spirit. We pray that this approach will guarantee great and sustained spiritual victory and continuation of our heritage.

CHAPTER I.
Holiness: Our Tradition Defined

The power and the presence of sin in the human life are deep-rooted and can only be effectively cleansed by the blood of Jesus Christ. While regeneration by faith in Jesus Christ deals with the initial communication of spiritual life by the Holy Spirit to a repentant sinner, the power of sin remains in control in the convert's life. The Holy Spirit, in His Pentecostal outpouring, has made full provision for the crucifixion of the "carnal" nature in order to fill the seeker with the nature and power of the Holy Spirit.

This necessary experience is recognized by several names including: holiness, entire sanctification, Christian perfection, the baptism with the Holy Spirit, the fullness of the Spirit and heart purity, among others.

This Biblically sound teaching was brought to Barbadian cities and villages as early as 1912, by overseas holiness missionaries as a distinctive of the North American holiness tradition. It was this gospel that gave birth to the now known Wesleyan heritage which this denomination embraces as it seeks to promote the power of God for national spiritual revival.

HOLINESS

In considering the understanding of holiness some persons may try to answer this question confidently, yet this is not usually the normal response today. "Holiness" is a noun that belongs with the adjective holy. The word "sanctify" means "to make holy. "Holy" means "separated and set apart for God, consecrated and made over to Him."[2]

Another definition of holiness is "a name used to express the state, condition, or quality of that which is holy. Used of God, it means holiness underived; of men, it means the moral quality of being holy...."[3]

> (a) Of God: Exodus 15:11 — "... who is like thee, glorious in holiness, fearful in praises, doing wonders?" "Holy, holy, holy is the Lord of hosts: the whole earth is full of his glory ..." (Isaiah 6:3).

> (b) Of Men: 2 Corinthians 7:1 — "Having therefore these promises, dearly beloved, let us cleanse ourselves from all filthiness of the flesh and spirit, perfecting holiness in the fear of God."

1 Peter 1:15-16 commands, "But as he which hath called you is holy, so be ye holy in all manner of conversation; because it is written, be ye holy; for I am holy."

Therefore, "Holiness is complete moral and spiritual purity. Wholeness, perfect soul health. This is a comprehensive term, implying godlikeness of character."[4]

ENTIRE SANCTIFICATION

The term entire sanctification is usually used alternatively with sanctification. Therefore, one needs to be aware of the theological

---

[2] Bruce Wilkenson, <u>30 Days To Discovering Personal Victory Through Holiness</u>, (Multnomah Publishers INC. 2003), p. 25

[3] Leslie D. Wilcox, <u>Be Ye Holy</u>, (The Revivalist Press, 1810 Young St., Cincinnatic, Ohio, 1965), p. 17

[4] Harry Jessop, <u>Foundations of Doctrine</u>, (The Free Methodist Publishing House, Winona Lake Indiana, 1946), p. 4

implications of the two terms in order to be clear, both in the use of the words, as well as in the experiences to expect and to teach.

Generally, some writers and preachers use the terms in reference to the act of the Holy Spirit in the life of the born-again Christian, to purify the life from the nature and practice of sin instantaneously.

However, in as much as it is taught by some Christian denominations that believers are baptized with the Holy Spirit at conversion or, in other terms, entirely sanctified at conversion, and since some others, including Wesleyans, teach that sanctification begins initially at conversion, it is incumbent upon us to know the differences.

CHRISTIAN PERFECTION

"Till we all come in the unity of the faith, and of the knowledge of the Son of God, unto a perfect man, unto the measure of the stature of the fullness of Christ:

"That we henceforth be no more children, tossed to and fro, and carried about with every wind of doctrine, by the sleight of men, and cunning craftiness, whereby they lie in wait to deceive...." (Ephesians 4:13,14)

This other term for holiness is not as ridiculous as it may appear. The term simply elevates the lifestyle of holiness to a standard, not of mediocrity but of spiritual excellency! The term does not claim:

    (1) Absolute perfection, which belongs only to the Sovereign God.

    (2) Angelic perfection, because man is not expected to be of an angelic nature.

(3) Adamic perfection, since man originally possessed a perfection unknown to man in his present state of existence.

(4) A perfection in knowledge. Inasmuch as man in his sinful state experiences perversion of his will, an alienated affection and a darkened intellect, then man is grossly affected in his nature and in his conduct with false judgment and biases.

(5) Immunity from temptation or proneness to sin.

It was Dr. H. Orton Wiley who believed, "Christian perfection is a spiritual constellation made up of these gracious stars: perfect repentance, perfect faith, perfect humility, perfect meekness, perfect self denial, perfect resignation, perfect hope, perfect charity for our visible enemies, as well as our earthly relations; and, above all, perfect love for our invisible God, through the explicit knowledge of our Mediator, Jesus Christ. And as this last star is always accompanied by all the others, as Jupiter is by his satellites, we frequently use, as St. John, the phrase 'perfect love' instead of the word 'perfection'; understanding by it the pure love of God shed abroad in the hearts of established believers by the Holy Ghost, which is abundantly given them under the fullness of the Christian dispensation."[5] Therefore, the word perfection must be understood in the context of being pure, undiluted, unmixed and utterly sincere.

THE BAPTISM WITH THE HOLY SPIRIT

Joel 2:28-30; St. Matthew 3:11; St. Luke 24:49; Acts 1:8; 2:1-19; Acts 15:8-9

The fact of sin in man's life is a problem for which no man has a solution; Wesleyan teaching declares that sin is not just what we do, but it is what we are by nature. Therefore, God's remedy for the cleansing of man's life from the power and practice of sin is

---

[5] H. Orton Wiley S., <u>Christian Theology, Volume II.</u>, (Beacon Hill Press, Kansas City MO., 1966), pp. 496-497

through the baptism with the Holy Spirit. This was proclaimed by John the Baptist in St. Matthew 3:11, "I indeed baptize you with water unto repentance: but he that cometh after me is mightier than I, whose shoes I am not worthy to bear: he shall baptize you with the Holy Ghost and with fire." John the Baptist was declaring his duty as the agent of water baptism, while Jesus, through the person and power of the Holy Spirit, will perform the spiritual task of immersion in the Spirit. "If what occurred on the Day of Pentecost was not the baptism with the Holy Spirit as promised by John, then John's promise was never fulfilled, for there is no other religious occurrence recorded in the New Testament which even approximates in power and depth that which occurred on the Day of Pentecost. When men are sanctified wholly, they are baptized with the Holy Spirit, and when they are baptized with the Holy Spirit they are sanctified wholly. One includes and implies the other."[6]

The baptism with the Holy Spirit is not simply a theological and traditional phrase used to associate this denomination with current church trends. It does represent the infilling of the Christian life with the person and the power of the Holy Spirit, who not only cleanses believers, but also saturates us with Holy Ghost power as we are immersed in the baptizing fire of the divine Spirit. This is what John Wesley experienced on Monday, January 1, 1739, at Fetter-lane's love feast with about sixty other brethren; as he states, "…'about three in the morning, as we were continuing instant in prayer, the power of God came mightily upon us, insomuch that many cried out for exceeding joy, and many fell to the ground…'; this outpouring of the Spirit upon this union meeting of the several Methodist societies seems to have been a profound turning point in Wesley's ministry. From then on he preached with unusual anointing and power…"[7] The baptism with the Holy Spirit releases holy fire deep within the soul of the believer for ministry.

---

[6] Richard S. Taylor, Life In The Spirit, (Beacon Hill Press, Kansas City MO., 1966), pp. 79-82

[7] Wesley L. Duewel, Ablaze For God, (Francis Asbury Press of Zondervan Publishing House, Grand Rapids Michigan 49506, 1989), p. 57

Rev. Dr. Carlyle Williams

THE FULLNESS OF THE HOLY SPIRIT

"Wherefore be ye not unwise, but understanding what the will of the Lord is. And be not drunk with wine, where in is excess; but be filled with the Spirit;" (Ephesians 5:17, 18)

While full salvation provides for both our pardon and our purity from sin, and inasmuch as regeneration deals with the forgiveness of our sins, the fullness of the Holy Spirit deals with the purging of our sin, termed the crucifixion of the "old man."

Jesus specifically admonished his disciples to wait at Jerusalem for the enduement, the clothing of their lives with Holy Ghost power from heaven which they needed for effective church ministry in order to turn the world upside down. Yes! It happened on the day of Pentecost. What a day in the history of the church! But Luke reminds us in Acts 4:31-33 of the possibility and necessity of the refilling of the fiery unction. The fire of the Holy Spirit was stirred by that special prayer meeting… "and they were all filled with the Holy Ghost, and they spake the Word of God with boldness… and with great power gave the apostles witness of the resurrection of the Lord Jesus: and great grace was upon them all."

The reality of the fullness of the Holy Spirit is in the fact that the Holy Spirit's presence and unction reside within the human body, which becomes the habitation of God through the omnipotent Holy Spirit. This holiness truth convinces me that every Spirit-filled saint is a mobile spiritual dynamo; a mobile spiritually active furnace! There is the functional presence of the Holy Spirit's power and purpose. Self is now replaced by the lordship of the Holy Spirit.

HEART PURITY Acts 15:8, 9

"And God, which knoweth the hearts, bare them witness giving them the Holy Ghost, even as he did unto us; And put no difference between us and them, purifying their hearts by faith."

Purifying in this context speaks directly to the function of cleansing, purging and purifying one's spiritual life from the nature of sin through the person of the Holy Spirit.

This very word is used in St. Luke 17:14 in the description of the cleansing of the ten lepers: "... they were cleansed." Even though the lepers were not made "Holy," there were indeed purged from their infirmity and restored to physical wholeness, including the removal of all the scars and defects caused by the leprous disease! "A heart that has been purified is no longer deceitful and wicked, but is sound and whole and clean in the sight of God."[8]

THE DOCTRINAL STATEMENT WITH RELEVANT SCRIPTURES

"We (Wesleyans) believe that Sanctification is that work of the Holy Spirit by which the child of God is separated from sin unto God and is enabled to love God with all his heart and to walk in all His holy commandments blameless. Sanctification is initiated at the moment of justification and regeneration. From that moment there is a gradual or progressive sanctification as the believer walks with God and daily grows in grace and in a more perfect obedience to God. This prepares for the crisis of entire Sanctification which is wrought instantaneously when the believer presents himself a living sacrifice, holy and acceptable to God, through faith in Jesus Christ, being effected by the baptism with the Holy Spirit who cleanses the heart from all inbred sin. The crisis of entire Sanctification perfects the believer in love and empowers him for effective service. It is followed by lifelong growth in grace and the knowledge of our Lord and Saviour, Jesus Christ. The life of holiness continues through faith in the sanctifying blood of Christ and evidences itself by loving obedience to God's revealed will."[9] Here are some relevant scriptural references for your study and memorization:

---

[8] Richard S. Taylor, , op. cit. p.66

[9] The Discipline of The Wesleyan Holiness Church 2003, (Wesleyan Publishing House, Marion Indiana, U.S.A. 2003), pp. 39-40

St. Matthew 5:8, 48; St. Luke 24:49; St. John 17:1-26; Acts 1:4-5,; 15:8, 9; Romans 8:3-4; 2Corinthians 7:1; Hebrews 10:14; 12:14

Dr. John W. Goodwin did a marvelous job as he defined entire sanctification as follows: "Entire Sanctification is a divine work of grace, purifying the believer's heart from indwelling sin. It is subsequent to regeneration, is secured in the atoning blood of Christ, is effected by the baptism with the Holy Ghost, is conditioned on full consecration to God, is received by faith and includes instantaneous empowerment for service."[10]

Paul summarized this glorious experience of holiness, in this lifetime, so marvelously when he declared to the saints of Ephesus that we, sinful men, were ordained to be the habitation or the dwelling place of God. This could only be done through the operation of the Holy Spirit, so that even the worst of Gentiles could be filled with "all the fullness of God" (Ephesians 3:19d). This is the quality of life which Wesleyans have experienced down through the ages, and which we are mandated by God to teach everyone with the purpose of spiritual change and personal victory over the practice of sin.

---

[10] H. Orton Wiley, op. cit. pp.468,469

CHAPTER II.
Holiness: The Nature of Our Divine God

"Holy, holy, holy, is the Lord of hosts: the whole earth is full of his glory ... for mine eyes have seen the king, the Lord of hosts." Isaiah 6:3(b), 5(d)

"Who is like unto thee, O Lord, among the gods? Who is like unto thee, glorious in holiness, fearful in praises, doing wonders?" Exodus 15:11

A. THE ABSOLUTE HOLINESS OF GOD

The Word of God declares Jehovah God as One who is absolute in holiness — the essential nature of His character, which aptly distinguishes Him as uniquely the Sovereign God: divine and transcendent, high and awesome. "It is of the very nature of God, the source and ground of all that is, to transcend, or rise above, His handiwork in majesty and glory ineffable. Thus, when a man is allowed to enter the immediate presence of God, he is stricken with some thing akin to terror. At the burning bush Moses takes off his shoes, and, before God in the Temple, Isaiah cries out in awe."[11] While Isaiah was favoured with the honour of beholding, in a snapshot fashion, a glimpse of God's majestic glory, it was only a glimpse of the Holy One of Israel.

---

[11] W.T. Purkiser, Exploring Our Faith, (Beacon Hill Press, Kansas City Missouri., 1960), p. 139

Moses desired to see God's face after Israel's worship of the golden calf. God's response was that no man shall see Him and live, but God offered him a compromise in allowing him to see His back. On Moses' second encounter with God at Sinai, God's glory, the splendour of His absolute holiness, overshadowed Moses to such an extent that on Moses' return to the Israelites' camp, he had to veil his face because of the radiance.

The absolute holiness of God was evident in the day of the high priestly administration in the temple: if sins were not confessed and atoned for by the appropriate sacrifice, the high priest was executed in the Holy Place! Sin was always punished instantaneously by God, if not covered by the appropriate sacrifice. Calvary demonstrates God's highest abhorrence of sin and God's powerful Holy nature. Therefore, it is man's highest honour to be cleansed by the blood of Jesus Christ and to be the abiding place in these times for the Holy Spirit.

B. THE MORAL EXCELLENCE OF GOD

"The Lord is righteous in all his ways and holy in all his works." Psalm 145:17

"...they rest not day and night, saying, Holy, holy, holy Lord God Almighty, which was, and is, and is to come." Rev. 4:8

"For a definition of holiness in God, we borrow the following statement from Lee's Theology (p.76): 'God is absolutely holy, because He possesses in His own nature all possible moral goodness to the exclusion of every kind and degree of moral evil."[12]

The holiness of God, as revealed in the Old Testament, demanded through the prophets justice, uprightness in conduct and integrity of attitude. Isaiah, God's prophet, demanded of Israel:

---

[12] Leslie D. Wilcox, Be Ye Holy, (The Revivalist Press, 1810 Young St. Cincinnati Ohio, 1965), p. 23

(1) Separation from their evil practices. Isaiah 1:16

(2) Separation unto justice and Integrity. Isaiah 1:17

(3) Confession of former sins. Isaiah 1:18

(4) Commitment to a future lifestyle of obedience to a Holy God.
Isaiah 1:19

Inasmuch as God's nature is absolute holiness, He demands as a principle for His creatures that same standard of moral excellence: Holiness. "... Be ye Holy: for I am holy" (1 Peter 1:16).

C. GOD'S DIVINE AUTHORITY TO COMMUNICATE HIS NATURE INTO THE REDEEMED

"Sanctify them through thy truth: thy word is truth." St. John 17:17

"That he might sanctify and cleanse it with the washing of water by the word...but that it should be holy and without blemish." Ephesians 5:26, 27c

"According as he hath chosen us in him before the foundation of the world, that we should be holy and without blame before him in love:"
Ephesians 1:4

The wonder of God's majesty sets Him up as the transcendent Ruler of the universe, yet His moral excellence and His absolute love shed His holiness into His sons, making us like Him: like Bridegroom, like bride (Ephesians 5:25, 26). What a God! An abiding Dweller within lives made holy by His power.

CHAPTER III.
Holiness: The Lordship and Leadership of the Holy Spirit

"And I brethren, could not speak unto you as unto spiritual, but as unto carnal, even as unto babes in Christ ... For ye are yet carnal: for whereas there is among you envying, and strife, and divisions, are ye not carnal, and walk as men?"
1 Corinthians 3:1, 3

Spiritual victory and ministry can only be possible through lives which are cleansed from sin and filled with the person and power of the Holy Spirit. Paul, in the above stated Scripture, identified the hindrance young converts experience in holy living: the lordship of the carnal spirit, the nature of sin, which continues to rule the life of the believer. This spiritual barrier has created great challenges and will continue to create greater challenges for the individual believer and the corporate church.

A. THE FACT OF THE CARNAL MAN

"... The 'law of sin' which is in my members." Romans 7:23

"... The body of this death ..." Romans 7:24

" ... With the flesh the law of sin" Romans 7:25

Paul's references stated in the above passages indicate the believer's obstacles to holy living and effective Christian service. The carnal man is that sinful principle which wars against the will of God; that strong enticement which undermines the Christian purpose and hinders noble performance. Romans 7:18-19 sets out Paul's painful struggle with the power of the self. "For I know that in me (that is, in my flesh) dwelleth no good thing: for to will is present with me; but how to perform that which is good I find not. For the good that I would I do not: but the evil which I would not, that I do."

The carnal man is that inherited evil bias in one's moral nature, not remedied by regeneration. The law of sin, the carnal man or the power of the flesh is the source of the painful spiritual conflict between the human and the Divine; the sovereignty of self and the Sovereignty of the Holy Spirit at war.

This experience of conflict hinders personal and corporate spiritual growth, as Paul highlighted in the church at Rome (Romans 7:18-25; 8:5-7), the church at Corinth (1 Corinthians 7 & 8), the church at Galatia

(Galatians 5:13-26; 6:1-10), the church at Ephesus (Ephesians 2:11-22; 5:8-21), and the church at Philippi (Philippians 4:1-9). Only when the Christian becomes aware of the terror of sin, enough to hate it, will there, like Paul, be the cry for help. Romans 7:24, "O wretched man that I am! Who shall deliver me from the body of this death?" This cry identifies the average Christian, who struggles with two patterns of behaviours and values, and who cannot experience consistent spiritual victory over the practice of his undesirable lifestyle."

- Man needs to be holy; it is God's will. 1 Thess. 4:3,4

- God ordained holiness for man as a bond of relationship. Ephesians 1:4, "He hath chosen us in him before the foundation of the world, that we should be holy and without blame before him in love."

- The carnal man is an enemy of God and spiritual life.

The carnal man is a perpetual enemy of God, the spiritual life and the progress of Kingdom building. Biblical holiness is God's solution for this subtle hindrance to man's acquisition of the fullness of spiritual blessings. Paul's spirit kept burning with disappointment as he identified his struggle with the 'body of sin'; as he labeled the Corinthian brethren as carnal who continued to fall back into works of the flesh even though they manifested certain gifts of the Spirit: the relational conflicts and divisions; their taking of some brethren to the law courts to resolve differences. It seems quite evident that the fact of the carnal nature does not go away, but rather demands death; it deserves crucifixion by the power of the Holy Spirit.

B. THE NECESSITY FOR THE CRUCIFIXION OF THE CARNAL MAN

The law of sin and death is the very principle of sin which Paul identified in Romans 7:23 as the hindrance to holiness. "God plans in Christ by the power of the Spirit to emancipate us from this inward proclivity which has been the cause of our defect."[13]

The law of the Spirit of life in Christ Jesus hath made me free from the law of sin and death" (Romans 8:2).

The law of emancipation from the slavery of sin and death.

The law of circumcision of the flesh. Colossians 2:11

The law of crucifixion of the old man. Galatians 2:20; "I am crucified with Christ: nevertheless I live; yet not I, but Christ liveth in me: and the life which I now live in the flesh I live by the faith of the Son of God, who loved me, and gave himself for me..."

---

[13] Richard S. Taylor, op. cit. p. 66

C. THE BAPTISM OF THE HOLY SPIRIT

Holiness as the lifestyle for the Christian, is a basic requirement of Jesus Christ for effective Christian conduct and service. St. Luke 24:49 proclaims the Messiah's promise of the Holy Spirit: "And behold, I send the promise of my Father upon you: but tarry ye in the city of Jerusalem, until ye be endued with power from on high."

Man is quite incapable of effective and fruitful spiritual ministry without the baptism of the Holy Spirit. Jesus, on the eve of His ascension, insisted that His disciples be energized through the baptism of the Holy Spirit before any attempt was made to perform any spiritual tasks. The principle Jesus was establishing for the church in every subsequent generation was to get clothed with the power of the Holy Spirit if any worthwhile service is to be done for Jesus Christ. This principle must be passed on by this generation of 2007 if the church is going to be on the leading edge for God's glory in the future.

The baptism of the Holy Spirit provides for heart purity, power for personal living in a polluted society, power for positive witness in a religious, lukewarm and pluralistic age. The church at Jerusalem in the first century was identified by an active and powerful prayer ministry. John Wesley's ministry was electrifying through the long hours he gave to prayer daily. The power of God bestowed through the baptism with the Holy Spirit is not an emotion as some believe; it is the release of an inner holy dynamic energy, an authority sustained by the commitment to waiting upon God in prayer. Therefore, some of the manifestations of the power of the Holy Spirit "may be summarized as follows:

- Power for personal living.

- Power for positive witness.

- Power In Prayer.

- Power for single hearted devotion or dedication to Christ.

- Power for Christian service."[14]

For as many as are led by the Spirit of God, they are the sons of God" (Romans 8:14).

D. THE PERSON OF THE HOLY SPIRIT

The endowment with and the leadership of the Holy Spirit are priorities for effective Christian witness in every age.

"Howbeit when He, the Spirit of truth is come, He will guide you into all truth: for He shall not speak of Himself: but whatsoever He shall hear, that shall He speak: and He will shew you things to come. He shall glorify me: for He shall receive of mine, and shall show it to you." St. John 16:13,14

Therefore, "...tarry ye in the city of Jerusalem, until ye be endued with power from on high" (St. Luke 24:49). Have you ever asked, "Who is the Holy Spirit?" He is the third member of the Godhead, sharing "the same essential nature, majesty, and glory as the Father and the Son, truly and eternally God. He is the Administrator of grace to all mankind, and is particularly the effective Agent in conviction of sin, in regeneration, in Sanctification and in glorification. He is ever present, assuring preserving and enabling the believer."[15]

---

[14] W.T. Purkiser, op. cit. pp. 387, 388

[15] The Discipline of The Wesleyan Holiness Church 2003, (Wesleyan Publishing House, Marion Indiana, U.S.A. 2003), p. 34

Rev. Dr. Carlyle Williams

THE PERSON OF THE HOLY SPIRIT: DEFINITIONS OF THE HOLY SPIRIT

1. THE THIRD PERSON OF THE GODHEAD

St. John 14:16-18 — "And I will pray the Father, and he shall give you another Comforter, that he may abide with you forever; even the Spirit of truth; whom the world cannot receive, because it seeth him not, neither knoweth him…I will not leave you comfortless: I will come to you."

Acts 5:3, 4 — "But Peter said, Ananias, why hath Satan filled thine heart to lie to the Holy Ghost, and to keep back part of the price of the land? While it remained, was it not thine own? And after it was sold, was it not in thine own power? Why hast thou conceived this thing in thine heart? Thou hast not lied unto men but unto God."

2. THE GIFT OF GOD TO THE CHURCH

"But ye shall receive power after that the Holy Ghost is come upon you: and ye shall be witnesses unto me…" Acts 1:8

"Then Peter said unto them, 'Repent, and be baptized every one of you in the name of Jesus Christ for the remission of sins, and ye shall receive the gift of the Holy Ghost.'" Acts 2:38

3. THE PRESENCE AND POWER OF GOD IN THE BELIEVER

"And when they had prayed, the place was shaken where they were assembled together; and they were all filled with the Holy Ghost…" Acts 4:31

4. THE WEAPON OF GOD AGAINST THE POWERS OF DARKNESS

"For though we walk in the flesh, we do not war after the flesh: (For the weapons of our warfare are not carnal, but mighty through God to the pulling down of strongholds;) casting down imaginations, and every high thing that exalteth itself against the knowledge of God, and bringing into captivity every thought to the obedience of Christ."
2 Corinthians 10:3-5

E. SOME BENEFITS OF THE ENDUEMENT WITH THE HOLY SPIRIT

1. PERSONAL REDEMPTION FROM THE DAILY PRACTICE OF SIN

Romans 8:4; Galatians 5:22-26; Ephesians 3:16-19

Regeneration is that act of God through the Holy Spirit which communicates spiritual life into a repentant sinner who was dead in sin. It is at this stage when one confesses one's sins. It is at this stage when one confesses one's deeds of previous sin. However, the nature of sin continues to rule one's life.

It is upon the struggling believer's request for deliverance from the body of sin and death that the Holy Spirit comes in His cleansing power and breaks the yoke of the flesh. The practice of holy love begins and the practice of sin ceases!

Paul challenged the Ephesian church to be careful about their lifestyle and to let it conform to God's pattern of the fullness of the Holy Spirit dwelling in their lives. Paul also challenged the Galatian church to cease the production of the fruit of the flesh by personal death to sin through the crucifixion of the old sinful nature. Paul was indeed outlining and insisting on the way out of spiritual inconsistency and constant spiritual failure. The practice of sin can be destroyed in this lifetime through one's surrender to the Lordship of the Holy Spirit.

2. PERSONAL PURITY AND AUTHORITY IN MINISTRY

Acts 1:8; 4:31-33; II Corinthians 10:3-7; Colossians 3:12-15; Ephesians 1:19-21

"The anointing with the Holy Spirit is a further aspect of this second work of grace – that which regards it as a conferring of authority and power. It refers, therefore, not to the negative aspect of cleansing, but to the positive phase of the indwelling Spirit as 'empowering the believers for life and service.'"[16] How often we have heard and read of the purifying work of the Holy Spirit with very little mention of the enabling power wrought in the ministry of those sanctified by the Holy Spirit. "The Spirit of God came upon David later when Samuel secretly anointed him King. Saul still wore the crown, but God rejected him from being King. Samuel anointed David, who had no crown. But the Holy Spirit came upon him immediately."[17]

The ministry of the Holy Spirit in the post-Pentecost church age purifies and empowers the believer for ministry as He dwells within a holy life! "... Wesley preached with such new authority and power that thousands came to the Lord. His journals, which he kept faithfully over the years, tell of people seized suddenly with tremendously deep Holy Spirit's power of conviction for sin. This account reminds one of Paul's experience when God's power struck him down on the road to Damascus. Under Wesley's preaching people often suddenly cried out aloud in great soul anguish ..."[18]

---

[16] H. Orton Wiley, op. cit. p. 324

[17] R.T. Kendall, <u>The Anointing: Yesterday, Today, Tomorrow</u>, (Charisma House, A Strange Company, Lake Mary Fla. 32746 U.S.A. 2003), p. 7

[18] Wesley L. Duewel, op. cit., p. 57

3. CORPORATE MINISTRY
Acts 2:42-47; Romans 12:3-21

The early church was full of spiritual vitality and urgency as they met daily in the temple or from house to house. There was corporate fellowship because of the Holy Spirit's control of the lives of the church family. Subsequent to the Pentecostal experience the disciples met daily in corporate ministry. They shared of their resources as they came together for Bible Study, prayer, the Holy Communion and brotherly encouragement. There was the practice of one-anotherness, commitment to the total well being of this new family circle: the family of the Spirit-controlled and Spirit-energized.

4. CORPORATE MATURITY AND CHURCH GROWTH
Eph. 4:11-16

The Holy Spirit equips the church in every age with the necessary ministry gifts for the total effectiveness of every member of the congregation. Jesus, the Chief Shepherd of the Church, provides for the Spiritual nurturing of His sheep. Therefore, spiritual gifts are not for adding any status to the Christian minister, but rather for the edification of the Body, the Saints of Jesus Christ.

Secondly, inasmuch as every Christian minister must function under the leadership of the Holy Spirit if there is to be any substantial impact upon those bound in sin, there must be personal empowerment through the Holy Spirit. The ministry of evangelism and deliverance is impossible without the supernatural enabling. Our church fathers throughout church history spent many hours in intercession, fasting and Bible study in preparation to minister to the lost: great was their success under the power of the Holy Spirit. Whether it was Stephen in Jerusalem, John Wesley in the British Isles or Dr. Wingrove Taylor in Barbados, their ministry of evangelism would be null and void without the mighty anointing of the Holy Spirit.

Thirdly, babes in the Christian faith must be nurtured unto maturity through consistent loving care and mentorship. Too many converts have slipped out of the Kingdom because of the lack of an effective system of follow-up care-giving. The church has got to look among its mature members for those spiritual teachers who ought to be recruited for the ministry of Christian development. If we are to see Church maturation and numerical growth, then we must be filled with the Holy Spirit, wisdom and commitment to Christian service.

F. THE LORDSHIP OF THE HOLY SPIRIT

1. THE ENTIRE POSSESSION OF THE CHRISTIAN BY THE LORDSHIP OF THE HOLY SPIRIT

Romans 12:1, 2; Eph. 3:14-19; 1 Thes. 5:23

2. THE INNER HABITATION OF THE SOUL BY THE HOLY SPIRIT

Eph. 5: 6-18; 1 Peter 1:11

3. THE SUBMISSION OF THE HUMAN WILL TO THE WILL OF THE DIVINE

Romans 6:19; 12:1; Galatians 2:20; Colossians 3:12-20

To submit: to put under the control of another.

Submission: the act of submitting.

"In our humanity we may strive to kill the monster of sin piecemeal, by striking off first this tentacle and then that. But it does not work that way. God's method is to deal decisively and crucially with self-willfulness itself. We may work for a while on jealousy, or possibly pride or anger, but all of these sins are but manifestations of a hidden, deep, underlying unsurrendered self. When the enemy is slain, the tentacles loosen their hold."[19]

Submission of the self will to the Divine will is the evidence of the death of sin in the human spirit through the sanctifying power of the Holy Spirit.

"I beseech you therefore, brethren, by the mercies of God, that ye present your bodies a living sacrifice, holy, acceptable unto God, which is your reasonable service." Romans 12:1

G. THE LEADERSHIP OF THE HOLY SPIRIT
Acts 13:2-4; Romans 8:14

When the Holy Spirit is Lord of one's life, then He is allowed to give leadership in one's life and affairs. He provides authoritative guidance to the submissive, sanctified saint.

"For as many as are led by the Spirit of God, they are the Sons of God." Romans 8:14

"The steps of a good man are ordered by the Lord." Psalm 37

SOME WAYS IN WHICH THE HOLY SPIRIT PROVIDES LEADERSHIP IN MINISTRIES AND OTHER VOCATIONS

The Holy Spirit is reliable in providing divine guidance for the Christian in life's ministries, vocations and in family life choices and

---

[19] Richard S. Taylor, op. cit., p. 85

Rev. Dr. Carlyle Williams

challenges. Therefore, as one commits oneself to the leadership of our Divine Counselor, he or she can expect His revelations.

a. Jesus' Earthly Ministry. St. Luke 4:1-21

Jesus' earthly ministry was completely empowered by the person and work of the Holy Spirit to whom Jesus continually committed himself. This example of Jesus is the powerful model for all who are in church ministry. There must be the call of God communicated by the Holy Spirit. There must be the separation by the called by the leadership of the Holy Spirit; and if there is going to be any fruitfulness in ministry there must be that notable companionship in service made known through the penetration of the power of God into the lives of those to whom we minister.

b. The Guidance of Saul of Tarsus into God's Purpose.

Acts 9:16 "For I will shew him how great things he must suffer for my name's sake."

Saul's conversion and consecration to Christian service must be and ever be that powerful manifestation of divine leadership in the affairs of men. Given Saul's passion for the Jewish traditions and his covenant to destroy any resistance to his way of life, it could have been God alone working through the person of the Holy Spirit who confronted and anointed Saul for God's master plan for this Saul! The Holy Spirit commissioned Ananias to anoint Saul; the Holy Spirit directed Barnabus to rescue Saul from rejection by the disciples. Yes! The Holy Spirit can be trusted to provide guidance into our divine destiny.

c. Philip's Ministry.

It is amazing to trace the spiritual journey of the deacon Philip. He was selected from among the disciples to provide care for the neglected widows in the early church. Then, as the persecution of that church increased, Philip went down to Samaria and was mightily used of the Holy Spirit in an historic revival. A church was born out of that revival, but Philip could not stay around to be the first pastor. Instead, the Holy Spirit moved him on to a remote village to witness to an African eunuch on his way back to Africa. This case seems so contrary to logic and to Philip's best interests. The principle here is: God was in charge of Philip's ministry and total destiny. This is the secret of spiritual success; this is the tradition which our fathers embraced: reliance upon the Lordship of the God of all wisdom.

d. The Church at Antioch.

The Church at Antioch was interrupted by the authoritative voice of God, directing the release of two of the most competent leaders in the congregation. However, Almighty God reserves the right to call us to what He sees best for us and His glory. Upon the obedience of Barnabus and Saul, there was a mighty Asian missionary invasion taking Jesus to the nation.

e. Other Vocations

The Holy Spirit does not only provide leadership in ministries, but He also equips His children in their life's vocations. Yes, He equips pastors, teachers, prophets, evangelists and apostles. He also equips business owners with the vision, courage and attitude to succeed in their gifted vocations.

What would family life be without the operation of the Holy Spirit's guidance in the choice of partners, in the development of understanding and Christian graces and the commitment to covenant relationship in marriage? God is equally committed to family life as He is to evangelism and church growth. Therefore, let the Holy Spirit have His control of our affairs as we partner with Almighty God.

CHAPTER IV.
Holiness: The Manner of the Experience

Holiness is God's method of purifying the believer's life from the problem of the flesh or the practice of sin. This experience is made possible instantaneously through the baptism with the Holy Spirit, who provides perfect soul health in exchange for the believer's surrender of his life by faith to God. "I beseech you therefore, brethren, by the mercies of God, that ye present your bodies a living sacrifice, holy, acceptable unto God, which is your reasonable service" (Romans 12:1). This position of instantaneous purity by faith is the Wesleyan's position as Scripture convinces us of a crisis experience. Simply put, one does not gradually grow away from the law of sin; as one is forgiven, redeemed or saved instantaneously by faith in Jesus Christ, one is equally baptized with the Holy Spirit in a single act of immersion in the Holy Spirit's power.

One other view of sanctification is that it is "the work of God's free grace, whereby we are renewed in the whole man after the image of God, and are enabled more and more to die unto sin and live unto righteousness."[20] Certainly, on the surface of this statement, there seems to be safety of truth, but the fact is death does not go on without end. Death is a crisis act! Even though one may be ill and on the road to death, there must be a distinct moment of death. Similarly, there is a historical time of death to the practice of sin in a believer's life.

---

[20] Kenneth Prior, <u>The Way of Holiness</u>, (Christian Focus Publications Ltd, Geanies House, Fearn, Ross-Shire Scotland Great Britain), p. 53

A. SOME SCRIPTURAL TERMS USED

1. THE ACT OF CRUCIFIXION

An act of punishment which culminates in death; a Roman form or manner of death for certain criminals. Similarly, "the old man must be kept on the cross until he dies; and when sin expires, in that moment the soul is entirely sanctified and lives the full life of prefect love."[21]

"Knowing this, that our old man is crucified with him, that the body of sin might be destroyed, that henceforth we should not serve sin." Romans 6:6

"I am crucified with Christ…" Galatians 2:20

2. THE ACT OF PURGING

The act of removing that which is impure and unnatural from one's spiritual nature.

"And he laid it upon my mouth, and said, lo this hath touched thy lips; and thine iniquity is taken away, and thy sin purged." Isaiah 6:7

"And put no difference between us and them purifying their hearts by faith." Acts 15:9

3. THE ACT OF DESTRUCTION

"We are commanded to "put off…the old man." Eph. 4:22

"Put on…the new man." Eph. 4:24

"Put away whatever belongs to the old, because we are now acknowledging only the new."

---

[21] H. Orton Wiley, op. cit., p. 483

You should have recognized that the scriptural terms identified all give very strong evidences of definite statements of time of action and the finality of said action: the act of crucifixion, the act of purging and the act of destruction. My argument is for crisis and not unending process.

B. SOME ENGLISH TENSES USED

"…when we come to consider the work of purification in the believer's soul by the power of the Holy Spirit, both in the new birth and entire sanctification, we find that the aorist tense is almost uniformly used. This tense, according to the best New Testament grammarians, never indicates a continuous, habitual, or repeated act, but one which is momentary and done once for all (e.g. St. Matthew 8:2, 3).

"And behold there came a leper, and he kept worshipping (imperfect) him, saying, Lord, if thou wilt, thou canst cleanse (aorist) me (once for all). And Jesus, stretching out (aorist) his hand, touched (aorist) him, saying, I will, be thou instantaneously cleansed (aorist)."[22]

"The leper prayed to be cleansed, not gradually, but instantly, and it was done at a stroke, according to his faith… Eph. 3:16-19. There are six aorists in four verses:

'grant,' 'be strengthened,' 'dwell,' (i.e. take up his abode)

'may be able to comprehend,' 'to know,' 'be filled.'"[23]

These English tenses have been highlighted to justify the principle of crisis, action at the stroke of the release of faith in the operation of the Holy Spirit for either physical or spiritual cleansing.

---

[22] Harry E. Jessop, op. cit., p. 88

[23] Ibid., p. 88-90

C. SOME THEOLOGICAL TESTIMONIES PRODUCED

"Those who teach that we are gradually to grow into a state of Sanctification, without ever experiencing an instantaneous change from inbred sin to holiness, are to be repudiated as unsound – antiscriptural and anti-Wesleyan" (Nathan Bangs, in *Guide to Holiness*). "Though purity is gradually approached, it is instantaneously bestowed"[24] (Bishop Hamline).

"Virtually all Bible believing Christians recognize that justification or the new birth is an experience which is not gradual but instantaneous. It is an act of divine grace which takes place at a given point in a believer's life. But if both Justification and Sanctification are products of the same divine love, the same will of God, the same Holy Word, the same blessed Spirit, the same redeeming Blood, the same marvelous grace, and are in answer to the same human condition, faith – is there any valid reason for supposing that one is instantaneous while the other is gradual?"[25]

If Adam by one sinful act plunged the entire human family into spiritual chaos, couldn't the second Adam, Creator and Sustainer of the universe redeem and sanctify believers by their exercise of faith instantaneously? Certainly, our God is quite capable and indeed that is His mission and unique action.

Our Church fathers challenged their congregations to surrender their old nature, their wills, their total lives to the power of the Holy Spirit for the purging of their sinful nature by the blood of Jesus Christ. As faith was released by the saints as they held on in prayer, victory was confessed. Even today as you surrender your weaknesses and shortcomings to the Master, you can experience the fullness of the Holy Spirit instantaneously by faith in the miracle working power of the Divine Sanctifier!

---

[24] H. Orton Wiley, op. cit., p. 482
[25] W.T. Purkiser, op. cit., p. 356

CHAPTER V.
Holiness: Our Tradition Became Our Holiness Heritage

"And God, which knoweth the hearts, bare them witness, giving them the Holy Ghost even as he did unto us; And put no difference between us and them, purifying their hearts by faith." Acts 15:8-9

The choice to forsake one's home, country and other comforts in life in order to take the gospel to another country and another culture, with the added challenges which a small island of minimum economic resources has to offer, is indeed an invaluable contribution — an investment for eternity.

1. THE DEVELOPMENT OF OUR BARBADIAN HOLINESS HERITAGE

A. MINISTRY THROUGH OVERSEAS MISSIONARY LEADERS

Thank God! They chose Barbados: Rev. C.O. Moulton, who it is stated was mightily owned and blessed of God in ministry here on the island, who was later followed by Rev. James M. Taylor with an evangelistic party. However, it was in 1912, "under the superintendency of Rev. Ralph G. Finch, a nucleus for our first local church was found among those who had been gathered in and through the ministry of the early missionaries. The loyal saints who had faithfully held together following the

Rev. Dr. Carlyle Williams

lamented death of our beloved Bro. Moulton rallied to the cause of holiness...."[26]

It was four years later, in 1916, that a Bro. James D. Tucker, "who had been saved and sanctified under the ministry of Rev. R. G. Finch and our missionary, Bro. Geo. Beirnes came from British Guiana to Pastor the work."[27] The Barbados holiness work was indeed on its wonderful journey, and the first Pilgrim Holiness Church was established officially in 1917, then known as the Whitepark Tabernacle, which indeed was the first Whitepark Church. Those early strides evolved out of the conviction that, "there is the need of evangelistic Pilgrim Holiness missionaries to minister to the spiritual need of the people of Barbados – 'to open their eyes, and to turn them from darkness to light and from the power of Satan unto God.'"[28]

Rev. & Mrs Wingrove Ives and children replaced Bro. Finch as District Superintendent in 1919. Rev. J.W. Humphrey, from the Immanuel Mission of Barbados, came to the Pilgrim Holiness with ten (10) of his churches, and members and were merged as one Pilgrim body in 1923.

The Spiritual development of the Holiness Church in Barbados was greatly enhanced by an outstanding lady. "Sis. Philomena Dummett, a Guyanese missionary, was one Pastor who contributed to the excellence of achievement by the church, during her service at the Carrington's Pilgrim Holiness Church from 1922-1936. Mother Dummett, as she is affectionately referred to, was born in Demerara on July 27th, 1894. Converted under the ministry of James Taylor, at the age of Sixteen..."[29]

---

[26] R. Wingrove Ives, <u>A Missionary's Cry From The Island of Barbados</u>, (Missionary Office, Kingswood, KY. U.S.A. 1930), p. 13

[27] Ibid., p. 14

[28] Ibid., p. 9

[29] J. Bend, <u>Historical Development of The Wesleyan Holiness Church</u>, 1978, pp. 10, 11

Mother Dummett was regarded as the most outstanding Pastor of the Carrington's Church, even when compared with stalwarts like Rev. L.S. Brathwaite, Rev. I.M. Wickham and Rev. C. West.

It is of great interest that within this denomination's first seventeen (17) years of ministry (1912-1929) it recorded its greatest spiritual harvest: "Twenty-nine mission stations in Barbados with a membership of twelve hundred and eighty-eight (1288) and a Sunday School enrollment of over twenty-five hundred (2500)"[30] It is significant that the Sunday School enrollment, which was twice the membership of the church, provided on a consistent basis the ripe harvest environment for evangelism and church growth. It is significant to note that, "A conservative estimate indicates that seventy-five percent (75%) of the members of all denominations come from the Sunday School. Eighty-five percent (85%) of all church workers and Ninety-five percent (95%) of all ministers and missionaries at some time were Sunday School pupils."[31]

Our Sunday School ministry experienced it's greatest harvest and enrollment between 1940 and 1945. This period provided stability for the church, the opportunity for spiritual teaching, discipleship, and the development of a lifestyle of holiness and enthusiastic evangelism not only within the church community, but also in adjoining parishes, because church planting continued across the island until most of the eleven parishes were served by a Pilgrim Holiness Church's ministry.

This writer must admit to the then-powerful impact of family life authority and its influence upon each child, whether in the home, at school, at church or in the marketplace. Children were very submissive to parental directives or they faced immediate reprimands. There was therefore powerful public school control and pastoral and church respect, even to the extent that prospective school teachers from the Pilgrim Holiness Churches were accepted

---

[30] R. Wingrove Ives, op. cit., p. 17

[31] Clarence H. Benson, Sunday School Success, (Indiana Pilgrim Publishing House, 1958), p. 11

with little difficulty by public school management, usually led by priests from the "state" churches (Anglicans and Moravians). There was a certain dignity attached to going to Sunday School and/or going to church. Even today, an adult who has not attended church for many years, when he hears of his former church, he would immediately raise his chin and declare, "I went to Sunday School at Whitepark Church as a boy, and it is still my church."

B. MINISTRY THROUGH BARBADIAN CHURCH LEADERS

The church growth experienced within the first seventeen (17) years of our history demanded parallel membership development through the knowledge of the Word and doctrine, Christian life and service. Inasmuch as the church membership was almost thirteen hundred and the Sunday School enrollment was fifteen hundred, workers were in demand. Open air services were very regular and effective, and indigenous lay workers were in demand. It is reported that by 1929 there were "around 100 local preachers and faithful exhorters, approximately ten percentage (10%) of total church population."[32]

Mother Dummett, who assisted Rev. J.D. Tucker at the Carrington's Church, was responsible for the Sunday School. Sis. Dummett was a people's developer. "Besides the regular services, they have a weekly young People's Bible Class, a women's meeting, a Vocal Music Class and a Teachers' Training Class."[33] The vision of Sis. Dummett was to invest in training and in developing young minds. Many of those young people became not only loyal members, but effective workers and ministers.

One of the first indigenous holiness stalwarts was a layman: Bro. Raymond Forde, formerly of the Immanual Mission. He was a preacher, church planter, sacrificial giver and deacon. Bro. Forde's

---

[32] R. Wingrove Ives, op. cit., p. 18

[33] Ibid., p. 29

passion for souls led him to borrow money on his sugarcane crops to purchase a building for a holiness worship centre at Massiah Street, St. John. The modern complex, which is being built now, has a lower sanctuary that was dedicated to the memory of, and in the name of, Raymond Forde.

Bro. Forde's investment at Massiah Street produced one of our greatest and spirit-controlled church leaders and preachers in the person of Rev. Prince Wiltshire. This church father wielded the Sword of the Spirit, the Word of God, fearlessly, firery and fruitfully. Men, women and children trembled under the anointed preaching of Prince Wiltshire. This mighty man of God — pastor, teacher of the Word, mentor, evangelist and musician — made a great impact on this entire nation. His ministry spanned over forty-three (43) years.

Furthermore, two other Immanuel Mission Churches which merged with the Pilgrim Holiness in 1923, Church Village and Ragged Point, were pioneered by Deacon Forde. "This station — Church Village — is the result of the labours of Deacon Raymond Forde, formerly of the Immanuel Mission. God has wonderfully blessed the ministry of this humble man of God. As our lay worker at this church, he nobly stands by Rev. Humphey, the Pastor."[34] This same comment was also the heartbeat with respect to the Ragged Point Immanuel Mission, now Wesleyan Holiness Church.

Even though Bro. Forde was not licensed as a pastor, his very ministry established him as an evangelist. Today's interpretation of an apostle by some scholars would classify Bro. Forde as an apostle. Whatever theological classification we attribute to this servant of God, considering the spiritual production of the churches under review, this brother has been a legend, a "Saint Paul" to the development of the faith and the Kingdom of God.

Tribute must also be paid to some other ministerial patriarchs, like Rev. Lewis S. Brathwaite. Very little has been recorded of this

---

[34] Ibid., p. 45

luminary who became the first national District Superintendent. Not even the date of the commencement of his tenure was recorded. However, my research revealed that Rev. Lewis St. Clair Brathwaite, a graduate of Codrington College, was appointed first national District Superintendent in 1932, as successor to Rev. Wingrove Ives.

Rev. L.S. Brathwaite recruited and tutored young Pilgrim laymen like Irvin Wickham, Colin West, Hezekiah Phillips and Prince Wiltshire. Pastor Brathwaite took such promising Pilgrim youths in his own care and prepared them for the pastoral ministry. So great was his influence that in 1936, when he was district superintendent, he went to Bro. Irvin Wickham's workplace on Roebuck Street in the city, where he also found Bro. Colin West, and appointed them on the spot, assigning Pastor Irvin Wickham and Assistant Pastor Colin West to the Sargeants Pilgrim Holiness Church. It is recorded that District Superintendent Rev. L.S. Brathwaite retired on February 1, 1938. He was a member of a well reputed family in the Barbados District.

Pastor Charles Wickham, affectionately known as 'daddy Wickham,' was another Pilgrim stalwart with his roots in the Immanuel Mission. He was in charge of the mission in Ellerton, St. George, until the merger with the Pilgrim Holiness in 1923. "Rev. W.M. Beirnes took over a little Baptist Mission here at Wobourne. Bro. Wickham stepped in and took charge and has laboured earnestly and successfully ever since."[35]

This man of God was also the father of Rev. Irvin M. Wickham, who even though deceased is still revered as a statesman — minister, pastor, teacher, the second national district superintendent and an international churchman and holiness champion. District Superintendent Wickham encouraged the training and the involvement of laymen in ministry. Young men were recruited and trained for pastoral service and challenged to aspire for excellence in lifestyle and ministry at the highest level as he led by example.

---

[35] Ibid., p. 44

The Rev. G. C. West could be referred to as the spiritual twin brother of Rev. I. M. Wickham. He was a meticulous electrician who utilized that same discipline in his ministry of people development. Rev. Hezekiah Phillips and Rev. G. W. Heywood, father of Rev. John Heywood, were the foundation layers of national reform through the propagation of holiness by lip and life.

The example of such indigenous spiritual champions gave to the then-Pilgrim Holiness ministry the leading edge in respect to integrity, transparency and authority of life, which are key evidences of the divine supernatural Lordship of life. Even unto this day, some senior saints speak longingly of those departed stalwarts of the Holiness Church. I salute our Abrahams, Moses, Joshuas and Barnabuses and Pauls. The then-Pilgrim Holiness Church was well respected in the Barbadian community.

It is of interest that District Superintendent Rev. L.L. Miller, at the 1940 Annual District Conference, issued this challenge: "In this last declining Laodician age there is a terrible tendency to count numerical additions and not genuine converts. Our need is a great spiritual awakening in the church as a whole and it must begin in the leaders, ministers, clerks and local workers and then to the membership, thus to the world. Let us pray to this end ... to gain this end of deeper spirituality and a revival awakening it will take more prayer, more fasting and more self-humiliation."[36]

C. MINISTRY THROUGH THEOLOGICAL TRAINING: CARIBBEAN PILGRIM/ WESLEYAN COLLEGE

The era of professional training of our church leaders commenced in Barbados very early in the 1950s. This was with the view of upgrading the church's quality and productivity in the pulpit as well as quality and productivity in the pew. Therefore, the Caribbean Pilgrim College was launched in 1951, and about eleven pastors

---

[36] H.A. Phillips, <u>Minutes of The Ninth Annual Assembly of The Pilgrim Holiness Church</u>, Barbados District, (Advocate Co. Ltd., Barbados, 1940), p. 11

from this district were enrolled. These adult ministers were exposed to the discipline of refinement in the manner, the method and the matter of spiritual leadership. Good leaders ought to be good learners. Paul, who was Timothy's mentor, exhorted him to "keep that which is committed to thy trust, avoiding profane and vain babblings, and oppositions of science falsely so called: which some professing have erred concerning the faith ..." (1 Timothy 6:20, 21). Spiritual leadership does not only require a clear vision and a systematic plan of action, but character, conviction, consistency and soundness of mind. Our holiness heritage was clarified, demonstrated and supported by the well selected and committed faculty and staff of Caribbean Pilgrim/Wesleyan College. Leaders can be made, but spiritual leaders are called by God, trained and commissioned with the awareness that they are accountable to the King of Glory. One former student, faculty member and pastor commented, "I found myself recalling how blessed my own life has been through the Christian influence of men and women who either taught me or studied with me at Caribbean Pilgrim College – Wesleyan College.

"I recalled the contributions such persons as J.W. Lashbrook, Gladys Dooley, W. Marshall, Ruby Christie, I.M. Wickham and others made to my life. I remember how they enriched my experience of holiness, my understanding of what it meant to be filled with the Holy Spirit and to be led by Him. Coming to Canada, the lives of those persons continued to inspire me, when it took me some time before I met fellow Christians who aspired to Biblical holiness, which is such a blessed part of my heritage."[37]

Ministry through the Theological training experience for that alumnus facilitated growth, maturation and a confidence necessary for the perpetuation of the Christian faith, which stirs and revolutionizes any society. Such testimonies create and establish the linkages necessary for the impact of the holiness heritage, for

---

[37] Vernon Smithen, <u>Caribbean Wesleyan College 50th Anniversary Souvenir Journal</u>, (Barbados 1992), p. 31

the essence of the Christian faith to be understood, desired and experienced at such a time as this post-modern era.

This Wesleyan community was favoured with quality ministry of the undergraduates of the Wesleyan College while it operated in this nation. Some students were enlisted in Christian education, whether as Sunday School workers, children's meetings directors, preachers, assistant pastors, evangelists or senior pastors. Even some of the college presidents served as pastors across this district. Consequently, a high quality of ministerial personnel engaged the minds of the laity: the youth, the adults and the community in general. With such a variety of personnel in ministry, learning was taking place; growth was visible and there was a special excitement to belong to the holiness church in the village and in the city. Visitors came to church with or even without any formal invitation because, in some cases, the constituents felt that the church was theirs even though they were not yet born-again and enrolled.

D. MINISTRY THROUGH BARBADIAN LAY WORKERS

Some Barbadian Lay Preachers

Historically, the lay worker in the holiness church referred specially to the church clerk or secretary, who functioned as the assistant pastor. His duty was to take full charge of the church in the pastor's absence, to visit and even administer the Lord's Supper to the shut-ins, to be responsible for the open-air services, and to keep the church record book up-to-date.

Another acceptance of the lay worker was the spirit-filled and loyal member whose preaching at the local level was approved by the local board and then made available to the district to be 'sent out' to other holiness churches to preach. In some cases, teams of members traveled to neighbouring communities, led by the church clerk in pioneer ministries and hospital ministries.

There were spiritually sound lay workers like Bro. Breedy of Social Hall/Dunamis, who donated the land for the church site; Bro. Oscar Worrell, known in some communities as 'Hell-Fire Worrell' because of the firey sermons; Bro. Ernest Gittens, Bro. Jeremiah Hall and Bro. James Carter, from the Kew/Mount of Praise church. Bro. R. A. Dear, one of the first members of the Whitepark Church, an outstanding liberal giver who also financially supported a local pastoral couple and a missionary in the then-British Guiana simultaneously, must be highlighted as a layman of great value. Some other early Whitepark stalwarts were Bro. C. Chadderton, Bro. Blackman, Bro. Crookendale and Bro. Harris. Another stalwart was Sis. Dorothy Millington of Chimborazo, pioneer of two churches, evangelist, youth developer, liberal giver, holiness pastor and mentor.

The Holiness legacy was handed to these lay workers who mobilized, propagated and enabled congregations, communities and families to experience the grace of God in the fullness of the Holy Spirit. In their own styles, these and other lay workers were mightily used in making disciples for growth of the church of Jesus Christ.

How can one forget the encouragement of a "God bless you" or, "I am praying for you" from those saints of our church family? Their sacrificial gifts of smiles, embraces, clothing or cash made holiness meaningful and functional. Indeed, life without such loving leaders, encouragers, chastisers and prayer warriors would have been spiritually aborted. These saints were not financially rich, but they had an intimate relationship with their Lord and so they were rich spiritually. That was all part of the inheritance transferred to their followers.

I must acknowledge the favour of God to this nation in general and to our denomination in particular, for purifying our hearts through faith in the power of the Holy Spirit as a direct consequence of the full gospel brought to us by obedient church leaders. Admittedly, the church, even though we commemorate some religious festivals, seems not to grasp the essentials for hilarious praise. "This failure will have its effects both in terms of what it has already done and what it is yet to do, despite any corrective measures. The loss of numerous opportunities to impart our faith and our heritage to younger generations and to impact more positively on our respective communities represents incalculable damage not just in terms of the past, but the future."[38]

2. THE DECLINE OF OUR BARBADIAN HOLINESS HERITAGE

"Now there arose up a new king over Egypt, which knew not Joseph." Exodus 1:8

A. A DEFINITE SHIFT FROM HOLINESS SERMONS

It was the late Rev. Frank Bailey who confessed that the foundation acquired in training at Caribbean Pilgrim College not only assisted in the development of his spiritual life but also equipped him in the difficult pursuit of 'higher education.' Furthermore, his pulpit ability and effectiveness as a preacher earned him great respect in

---
[38] Ibid., p. 21

his pastoral ministry in Canada, where he migrated. His service was soon engaged by his church leadership to re-establish courses in homiletics for the laity. His greatest joy was that seventeen (17) lay preachers were now serving across the United States and Canada because of the legacy of his exposure to discipline of his Barbadian alma mater. It was this Rev. Frank Bailey who was a student of Rev. I. M. Wickham and an assistant pastor to Dr. Wingrove Taylor: thus the heritage.

Regrettably, we have become victims of the global village "bug" with inadequate medication. The age of technology, the age of tolerance and the freedom of cross-cultural church bonding have become symbols of development. General Superintendent, Dr. Earle Wilson, of the North America General Conference, agreed with George Barna and James D. Hunter, as he quoted, "Not only are evangelical Christians more tolerant of behaviour contrary to what was euphemistically known as the 'five fundy sins of drinking, smoking, card-playing, movie-going and dancing, but their tolerance extends to theological ambiguity in regeneration and sanctification, relational breakdown in marriage and divorce and spiritual stewardship ... now comes the pressure to be tolerant of practices such as abortion, premarital sex and homosexuality...."[39]

With the background of a shifting holiness pulpit ministry, a modern aggressive living room television invasion of all kinds of sermons, and the inability to articulate Biblical holiness in sermon and in Bible study, the baton has already hit the track! The initiative has been transferred to the competitors.

These competitors also include the post-modern thinkers, the new social revolutionists and the new generation of parents whose value system is non-traditional. No wonder why so many children now seem to be in control of their parents. The family structure with its extended relationships has gradually deteriorated.

---

[39] Earle L. Wilson, Pastoral Letter, (Wesley Press Indiana U.S.A. 1996), p. 14

As a result, the holiness church in particular has been greatly challenged. Whereas parents once demonstrated maximum control over the discipline of their children, enjoyed closer relations as a family unit, and either brought or worshipped with their children at church, there is now a serious absence of many parents and children from church. With the Sunday sports and entertainment, the increasing shift in interest from the acceptance of the deity of Jesus Christ, and the virus of relativism, where every man can do as he wishes with no obligation to be accountable for his lifestyle, there is a greater demonstration of the impotence of conscience. Indeed, there is a new kingdom of pharaohs who despise the Joseph's characteristics — traditional values and progressiveness.

While holiness is a familiar biblical doctrine, only the trained eye is equipped to distinguish between the general subject and the specific truth of entire sanctification as the second definite work of the Holy Spirit. While it is popular to preach of the Spirit-filled life, the congregation needs to be told of the relationship between the Spirit-filled life and functional lifestyle holiness in the market place and in family challenges. Our fathers not only preached the fire of hell, but they also insisted on the experience of the fire of the Holy Spirit purging from sin and empowering the believer for ministry:

I am weakness, full of weakness,
At thy sacred feet I bow;
Blest, divine, eternal spirit,
Fill with power, and fill me now.
Fill me now, fill me now,
Jesus come and fill me now;
Fill me with Thy hallowed presence
Come O Come and fill me now.

Elwood H. Stokes

Rev. Dr. Carlyle Williams

Globalization is not only a socioeconomic and political philosophy, but it also has moral and theological implications. Therefore, as church leaders, our perceptions and revelations ought to be solidly grounded in biblical truth. Care must be taken that whatever is contrary must not be accepted in our pulpits; our heritage has got to be guarded through vigorous and regular public enunciations.

Rev. I.M. Wickham
The Second National District Superintendent 1962-1980.
An outstanding Church Statesman

B. THE STRONG IMPACT OF COMPETING SERMONS UPON BARBADIAN HOLINESS MEMBERS

A weak pulpit will produce weak members. It is well known that man is a creature of his environment, and when we are more exposed to error delivered in an aggressive style and with passion, there is a tendency to accept that information without question.

The Internet ministry is very powerful, and while there are volumes of worthwhile information on the Internet, there is an equal volume of spurious information as well. Many modern Bible teachers, evangelists and pastors are being informed through the Internet. If that information is not critically analyzed before it reaches the pulpit, the youth meetings and the Sunday School classes, you can image the extent of the spiritual damage.

There is an increase of gospel preachers on local radio stations, and there are some whom I have to turn off and warn others about. I also remind pastors to carefully select those preachers who are allowed to fill their pulpits. The strong currents of ecumenicalism, trans-denominationalism and religious tolerance are too deceptive and deadly. Unfortunately, the time has come when holiness leaders such as this writer have got to defend our holiness heritage even against some Wesleyan preachers. This ought not to be the case, but it does signal the serious decline in the understanding of and the loyalty to biblical holiness as proclaimed by John Wesley and as we understand through experience with the Holy Spirit.

C. THE DEFINITE LACK OF A CONSISTENT SYSTEMATIC TEACHING MINISTRY IN ALL LOCAL CHURCHES

One area of great need in our holiness ministry is a greater cadre of Bible teachers. Many church members have expressed their need for more Bible study in their assembly. The Old Testament patriarchs were mandated to use specific educational tools for the teaching of the Word — Bible Study. "And these words which I command thee this day shall be in thine heart: And thou shalt teach them diligently unto thy children, and shalt talk of them when thou sittest in thine house, and when thou walketh by the way, and when thou riseth up. And thou shalt bind them for a sign upon thine hand and they shall be as between thine eyes..." (Deuteronomy 6:6-8).

This Jewish method of becoming acquainted and conversant with the law of God was to memorize, repeat in word, in chants and in group interaction in order to enhance the learning process. Even though this method referred to a recommended teaching method for children in Jewish homes, it has been adopted by modern educators in the local school system. One might question why the church should not adopt this biblical method as a desirable tool, as a developmentally appropriate practice to ensure the desired spiritual development in the basic doctrines of the church, particularly to the young. Yes, the sermon has its place in public ministry, but inasmuch as it does not allow for questions and responses, we must put in place the relevant educational tool for the desired effect. No church will be as productive as desired until it has teaching teachers and learning pupils or members. The public schools are not basically Christ-centred agencies, but they utilize a biblical methodology. Let the church rise up and be on the cutting edge of Christian education in order to reverse the decline in the development of basic holiness truth in teaching the youth and beginners in the faith.

Furthermore, the Local Board of Administration of each church should employ a consistent process of prayerfully analyzing membership growth through discerning graces and gifts suitable for the selection of candidates for training — not only as teachers for the Sunday School, but also as Christian educators within the local church — in order to achieve positive ministry goals. The holiness church must invest its greatest resources in the declaration of its central message. "Except a corn of wheat fall into the ground and die, it abideth alone: but if it die, it bringeth forth much fruit" (St. John 12:24). Let us strive to preserve our heritage by a consistent systematic teaching ministry.

D. THE INABILITY OF MANY YOUTHS TO ARTICULATE CONVINCINGLY OUR HOLINESS HERITAGE

"Evil men and seducers shall wax worse and worse, deceiving, and being deceived. But continue thou in the things which thou hast learned and hast been assured of, knowing of whom thou hast learned them; and that from a child thou hast known the holy scriptures which are able to make thee wise ... through faith which is in Christ Jesus ... that the man of God may be perfect ..." (II Timothy 3:12-17).

Paul, the astute Christian leader and teacher, sought effectively to mentor young Timothy, in particular, through the teaching and application of sound biblical principles against the then-current social and religious landscape of moral decadence, religious error and intense spiritual darkness. Such a culture seems to be spreading in our land today.

Paul was mature and personally evaluated the cultural, social and religious attacks on his faith and life, enabling him to speak to Timothy from a position of personal experience. His charge to Timothy was sound and guaranteed to work.

Today's spirit of rampant materialism and relativism has inflicted severe damage upon family life and religious behaviour in the world in general, but particularly upon our small developing nation. The plagues of abortion, H.I.V and Aids Virus, sexual promiscuity and illegal drugs are all with us, and our youth are the main targets. The central person of the holiness message is the Holy Spirit himself. Paul assured Timothy of the power of God's Word — the power of faith in that Word which makes the man of God perfect. That is the message, in summary, of personal Christian perfection or heart purity. This is God's weapon offered to man against satanic giants of any age. As Paul wrote in Ephesians 6:12, "For we wrestle not against flesh and blood, but against principalities, against powers, against the rulers of the darkness of this world, against spiritual wickedness in high places."

Furthermore, Paul's exhortation to Timothy to acquire the knowledge of the Holy Scriptures, gives promotion to Christian education and its related benefits in a spiritually challenged society such as ours. charts A and B reveal a serious decline in our church school enrollment as well as in the church school's averages over the last five (5) years at two (2) of our larger churches. Whereas, these same churches on chart A registered enrollments between 300 and 412 students between 1940 and 1945, such church school enrollments were higher than the church membership roll. Chart B registers a declining Sunday School enrollment and, to a large extent, a declining church membership. In those early years, there was no exposure to the teaching aids, electrical technology, nor such physical facilities offered currently, yet there was consistent production both in the schools and in the church growth. It seems very clear that whenever the Sunday School enrollment was higher than the church's membership, very often the church membership kept growing.

Whatever contributed to the rapid current decline in our church school and church membership rolls did not only affect numerical growth but, most significantly, aborted the spiritual development of many of the young people. Consequently, a great percentage of the prospective stewards of the gospel was lost to the church family and the church mission of holiness. The ability to memorize, to recall or to discuss scriptural truth is no longer a strength of our youth; traditional values are greatly ignored and our day school system appears to be morally out of control. My submission is that the place and the power of Scripture within the minds and spirit of the youth being absent in the society as a whole leaves our youth defenseless to attacks of the seducer and to the destroyer of spiritual life. Satan is his name!

Rev. L. L. Miller, that former spiritual visionary and district superintendent of our denomination, declared in his 1939 annual report that, "A spirit-filled, fire baptized ministry... will permeate every pulpit, fill every pew and energise every worker and lay member ... Let us again set these three goals for the coming year: Personal holiness for every member of the Pilgrim Holiness Church; a vitalized, burden-bearing soul travail and an urge to seek the lost where they be found; the tithe as God's method of church finance."[40] Even as Rev. L.L. Miller, now deceased, proclaimed in

---

[40] H.A. Phillips, Minutes of The Eighth Annual Assembly of The Pilgrim Holiness Church, Barbados District (Advocate Co. Ltd. 1939), p. 14

1939 such an accurate divine solution for our infant church renewal, it still remains the solution for today's adult church's renewal. That was the challenge of Christ to His disciples as He departed this earth and handed to them the leadership of the emerging church two thousand (2000) years ago with the following promise: "But ye shall receive power, after that the Holy Ghost is come upon you: and ye shall be witnesses unto me both in Jerusalem, and in all Judea, and in Samaria, and unto the uttermost part of the earth." Acts 1:8

CHAPTER VI.
Holiness: The Proclamation of Our Holiness Heritage Through Systematic Teaching

Preaching has its place in the development of the church and the kingdom of God. The denomination's history bears witness to this fact. Preaching is the spoken communication of divine truth with the express purpose of persuasion. A preacher under the fullness of the Holy Spirit is irresistible, because it is the Holy Spirit himself on duty in the pulpit as well as in the pew. "God's answer to a cold world of indifference, materialism, coldness and mockery is burning Christian hearts in pulpits, in pews, in Sunday Schools, in Bible Institutes, and in Christian colleges and seminaries ... if we are to be an irresistible force for God where He has placed us, we need the Spirit's baptism of fire. If we are to awaken our sleeping church, we need the holy flame that came upon each waiting believer in the upper Room to descend upon us today ..."[41]

Where the church has fallen short of the great commission of Jesus Christ is in its failure to utilize the ministry of teaching as it utilizes the ministry of preaching. It has failed in the entire ministry of Christian education: in the Sunday School, which provides for all ages, in the family unit and in the corporate church assembly, which mainly uses the preaching medium rather than teaching for the proclamation of biblical truth.

---

[41] Wesley L. Duewel, op. cit., pp. 27-29

Rev. Dr. Carlyle Williams

The church needs this ministry of teaching to guide the youth into the path of holiness as early as possible. Consider the example of Jesus our Master Teacher.

A. JESUS: THE MASTER TEACHER

Jesus prayerfully selected his disciples for the ministry of Kingdom development. Each disciple brought a special characteristic to the team. Jesus worked with their strengths and weaknesses in the three year developmental process. It is very significant to note that, "Jesus taught as He did, I think, much like Socrates, because He was more concerned with eliciting insights and responses from his disciples than with imparting rigorously structured, detailed content. He proclaimed the truth that both liberates and captivates those who see it ... He tried, it seems, to guide His disciples to the place where they could see and thus truly know."[42]

Jesus was the master discipler. He was not just interested in presenting a lesson or passing on information, but in the development of a personal knowledge of God and His team for life service; Jesus was training trainers. He spent 80% of his time on the most promising 20% of the potential leaders around him. This developmental programme is ably explained by Dr. John C. Maxwell, who shares a five-step process for training leaders.

I model by doing the task, while the trainers watch. When they see the task done professionally they are motivated to duplicate. Step two involves the leaders' continuation of the task, but now it engages the assistance of the trainee. This is the mentoring stage. "We exchange places this time. The trainee performs the task and I assist and correct ... once he's gotten done the process, ask him to explain it to you."[43] The two other vital stages are the motivational, where the trainee is encouraged to add any personal idea and share

---

[42] The Preacher's Magazine, (Beacon Hill Press Kansas City MO. 641091 1986), p. 45

[43] John C. Maxwell, Developing Leaders Around You, (Thomas Nelson Publishers Nashville Tenn. U.S.A. 1995), pp. 99-101

it with the teacher. The final stage is for the trainee to teach others. This stage is the multiplier — developing your own trainees.

Jesus selected His disciples with the purpose of sharing the responsibility of leadership, investing His disciples with the authority to perform with competence and confidence. Their challenge was that even though they were entrusted to function, they were aware that they were accountable to their trainer and leader. This was the mission of Jesus as the Master Teacher as he trained his staff for three (3) years.

B. THE PASTOR: THE PRIME TEACHER IN THE LOCAL CHURCH

Rev. Dr. H. Taitt
The Third National District Superintendent 1981-1986.
Bible Teacher and Preacher

The Pastor is expected to be the visionary and inspirational leader for the local congregation. In order for the local church to rise to the challenge of effective Christian education, there must be a passionate urgency within the spiritual bowels of the Pastoral leadership. "...When he saw the multitudes, he was moved with compassion on them, because they fainted, and were scattered abroad, as sheep having no shepherd" (St. Matthew 9:36). The current spiritual challenges must be confronted with a thorough training ministry in each local church especially developed with the children, youth and recent converts in mind.

The social problems and the shallow Christian behaviour demand of the church an urgent and systematic indoctrination ministry. Our teaching must enlighten the minds, extinguish the darkness and empower wills to perform with new character reflective of the presence of the divine authority of Christ as Lord of our lives.

C. SELECTION AND DEVELOPMENT OF CHRISTIAN EDUCATION STAFF

"… Look ye out among you seven men of honest report, full of the Holy Ghost and wisdom, whom we may appoint over this business." Acts 6:3

One special target group must be the youth and the new membership of the church family. The youth have special emotional, moral and spiritual needs, which must be planned for within their age grouping and through trained competent and compassionate staff. This crop of wonderful and precious leaders for the future has got to be nurtured through loving tender care, prayer and an effective teaching programme.

1. SELECTION OF CHRISTIAN EDUCATION STAFF

The early church observed a selection policy in its plan to discover and appoint persons of the highest quality to serve in the business of the Kingdom. This principle must become the benchmark in these times for the recruitment of Christian education staff. There are too many complaints about teachers' lack of passion for the children's well-being, lack of zeal for visitation, indiscipline and lack of people skills. The Local Church Board, in order to select quality staff, must identify and implement quality standards.

"Leaders cannot rise above the limitations of their character."[44] The Local Board of Administration must include in its list for prospective teachers such characteristics as: total commitment to Christ as well as commitment in general, character, charisma, courage, teachability, self-sacrifice and communication skills. We must always remember that the Christian education department will never perform above the limitations of its leaders. "Many people regard leaders as naturally gifted with intellect, personal forcefulness and enthusiasm. Such qualities certainly enhance leadership potential, but they do not define the spiritual leader. True leaders must be willing to suffer for the sake of objectives great enough to demand their wholehearted obedience ... one does not become a spiritual leader by merely filling an office, taking course work in the subject ... a person must qualify to be a spiritual leader."[45] Therefore, inasmuch as the best persons must be recruited for training as spiritual leaders in the Christian education ministry, it must be considered that there can be no shortcuts to efficiency.

Furthermore, the Local Board of Administration ought to employ a consistent process of prayerfully observing the growth of members, discerning graces and gifts and suitability for the selection of the teaching staff. Inasmuch as there is an obvious need for excellent staff, let us be involved in an ongoing process of recruitment.

2. DEVELOPMENT OF CHRISTIAN EDUCATION STAFF

So many of our church members have experienced several hours of ongoing training in order to be on the leading edge in their work places. In many cases, such training sessions are not optional and the church members submit to authority in the work place: this is

---

[44] Ibid., p. 5

[45] J. Oswald Saunders, <u>Spiritual Leadership</u>, (Moody Press, 1994), p. 18

Christian and commendable! However, this attitude is also desirable and required in God's business centre: the church of Christ! "Sunday School workers should avail themselves of every means of improvement and growth. This means that they should go to conventions and training schools ... and when they return should pass on the good things they have learned to the other officers and teachers in the school."[46] We need to be convicted by the truth that the teacher is God's messenger of the most important news, which is required for bringing each student into his/her life's purpose.

"The president of a great state institution of learning said, in the writer's presence, on one occasion, that, in his judgment, the teacher counted for eighty-five percent of an education and the curriculum or subject matter taught, for not over fifteen percent."[47] Jesus, in His great commission charged his graduating disciples to go into all the earth and TEACH all nations. Therefore, in order to teach others we must first submit our attitudes, our minds and our schedules to the discipline of being a student.

Teachers, who are responsible for the transfer of information through education, must be constant learners. It must be remembered that when one ceases to learn, then one ceases to teach, because the teacher must always be tapping new springs of teaching methods and teaching aids, and he must be familiar with new technology in order to be relevant and on the leading edge in the teaching profession. In this age of advanced teaching methods, the strategic importance of teacher training has become even more challenging and vital. The lecture method of teaching is easier for the teacher but is a turn-off for students. Teachers must reach and retain the student's mind and interest as well as sustain a passionate hunger for fresh ideas.

My research extracted from a church member her conviction that teachers and children's ministry personnel ought to be trained in

---

[46] Marion Lawrence, <u>My Message To Sunday School Workers</u>, New York: Harper and Brothers Publishers, 1924), p. 29

[47] Ibid., p. 53

methods of understanding the behavioural makeup of children: what caused them to do the things they do at their age. What an observation! A very critical observation, yet the District Christian Education Director has been offering an ideal course of study to all Sunday School workers with minimal response. The Local Boards of Administration have to enforce a training policy in the best interest of change of teachers' attitudes and development skills.

D. BASIC PROGRAMMES OF STUDY

"A well-planned, carefully executed, long range training program is a proven method of building a successful Sunday School by eliminating the major problem of the average, unproductive school. No Sunday School is really a "school" unless it has teaching teachers and learning pupils. Trained teachers are important. They are more successful. They do a better job."[48]

It is noteworthy that the public school system, although not Christ centred, pursues a biblical methodology. This may be totally unknown to the public school system but very true nonetheless.

THREE COMMENDABLE MODERN EDUCATIONAL METHODS

There are three commendable modern educational methods that reflect biblical principles and are useful in the church's ministry to children: Life Related Lessons, Early Childhood Education and Developmentally Appropriate Practice. Our teachers must be trained to appreciate and to promote active involvement in the learning process and to teach students to relate lessons to life.

> (a) Life Related Lessons are a modern educational tool which derived its significance and effectiveness from the divine principle revealed to Moses and was used by the Jews in their educational system. "And these words which I command

---

[48] Clarence Benson, <u>Sunday School Success</u>, (Indiana, Wesley Press, 1978), p. 58

thee this day shall be in thine heart: And thou shall teach them diligently unto thy children, and shalt talk of them when thou sittest in thine house, and when thou walketh by the way, and when thou riseth up…" (Deuteronomy 6:6, 7).

This Jewish method of becoming acquainted and conversant with the law of God was to memorize, to repeat, to chant, to discuss, to write and to post in strategic places, even on their bodies, in order to enhance the learning process. The Jewish child's life was marked by festivals, celebrations and the repetition of the relevant rituals. Whenever a particular festival was drawing near, the appropriate preparation was made, including the revision and rehearsal of rituals. Therefore, it was very easy for the Jewish children to be familiar with what was taught.

Similarly, modern educational methods reflect those traditional and proven Jewish principles, such as memorization, discussions, active participation by doing, action songs and maybe dance, repetition and the use of charts.

(b) The second modern educational method is Early Childhood Education. There is an old Roman Catholic principle which, in essence, states that if you give a child to the Catholic Church for its first seven (7) years, that child remains a Catholic for life. This principle highlights the power of the innocent and fertile child's mind. If it were a fact that a child learns fastest within its first seven (7) years, then "train up a child in the way he should go, and when he is old he will not depart from it" (Proverbs 22:6).

Modern educators, with their training and experience, are encouraged in the promotion and in the use of Early Childhood Education in church ministry.

(c) The third modern education method reflective of biblical principles is Developmentally Appropriate Practice. "Both scripture and modern educational theory emphasize the importance of Developmentally Appropriate Practices. Lesson contents and teaching methods must be geared to the student's level of understanding."[49] Paul, the renowned early church teacher, declared, "I fed you with milk and not with solid food; for until now you were not able to receive it" (I Corinthians 3:2). Evidently, Paul kept evaluating the growth process of each church based on its learning capacity.

Modern educators have defined the human process of development physically, mentally, socially, emotionally, and spiritually with the relevant age grouping, needs, characteristics and behavioural patterns so that the teachers of any age group can effectively prepare and present adequate lessons. Similarly, the Christian Education ministry, when it incorporates Life Related Lessons, Early Childhood Education and Developmentally Appropriate Practice into our Sunday School ministry, can enable our nation's children to increase in wisdom, in stature and in favour with God and man.

THE IMPORTANCE OF UNDERSTANDING A CHILD'S DEVELOPMENT

Man is fearfully and wonderfully made. The human body and a person's emotional development are distinguished by patterns and stages. "It is possible to recognize patterns and stages in human growth and development. These patterns of development help clarify needs and aid leaders to serve people."

Our Sunday School staff also must be trained in the art of understanding a child's development. "One area of education in

---

[49] Robert J. Choun & Michael S. Lawson., The Christian Educators Handbook On Children's Ministry, (Michigan: Baker Book House Co., 1998), p. 31

which Christians can and should use available research is child development."[50] Researchers over the years have been observing children and have established measurable standards to gauge the development of children. These standards are divided into three categories: Physical Development, Social and Emotional Development and Mental and Spiritual Development.

(a) Physical Development.

It is said that the chief business of the infant is to grow. Given the appropriate nutrition, exercise and sleep, the infant quickly outgrows the nursery and demands more space. Activity will lead to growth and development; while the body is growing, development is also taking place. Development, it is said, "implies change in the character of the body which makes for maturity and strength ... the body ... also develops the senses and the intellect. The child gradually perceives and understands through impressions gained by touching, tasting, smelling and hearing."[51]

Development patterns vary greatly: girls shoot ahead of boys in statue and in maturity, but eventually the boys catch up with the girls. As they both reach adolescence, their bodies once again experience significant changes in preparation for parenthood.

(b) Social and Emotional Development.

The infant's world is limited to its home environment which is a composition of the immediate family circle. The child explores and adapts himself to his world. This adventure is done by gaining attention through sounds, gestures and actions; at the same time the child is building relationships and also becoming sensitive to its surroundings. It begins

---

[50] Ibid., P.31

[51] J. Omar Brujaker & Robert G. Clarke, Understanding People, (Indiana, Wesley Press, 1977), p.22

to learn and appreciate the safety of mother's care while it develops caution with strangers.

As the infant grows and develops through the expansion of its society, confidence and a gradual sense of independence will be gained. Other children and adults begin to broaden the territory of the child. Trust, cooperation, friendship and play become a prominent part of their new world.

This socialization programme is accelerated as the child enters nursery school. Life takes on the challenge of choosing playmates, getting to understand the opposite sex of its age group and the recognizing behavioural differences. Before the parents realize what is happening, the child is now asserting its independence in choosing friends and making demands as a teenager.

(c) Mental and Spiritual Development.

Man is heavily influenced by his environment, and with the added blessings of God-given senses, his exploration of his world begins very early in infancy. The use of the senses of smell, touch, taste, hearing and seeing inform the mind and the inner desires. Isn't it true that sometimes, we adults are alarmed by our children's questions?

Equally significant is the existence of the divine presence in the home, which can enhance the spiritual development of the child. The impact of this domestic culture, when displayed with consistency and love as a lifestyle, enhances great spiritual sensitivity to the development of the attitude of obedience to the Word of God.

The teacher, having received training in the systematic development of children, is better able to understand the child's characteristics and needs and has the knowledge to prepare and present an effective lesson. There is a great principle which states, "Children will not actively apply what they have been passively taught... The more of the five senses that an activity utilizes, the greater the learner's involvement and rate of retention. Research has proven that learners remember only 10% of what they hear and only 20% of what they read... the combination of both seeing and hearing pushes the percentage all the way to 50% ... The learner who not only can talk about a concept in his own words but can also be actively involved in learning it will retain a whopping 90%!"[52]

The research undertaken for this thesis has revealed the urgency for this Wesleyan Holiness Church to recapture the holiness tradition and to transmit the holiness heritage to this generation and others beyond. It was very disappointing to hear some of our outstanding young adults sharing their concerns about the need for systematic preaching and teaching of fundamental doctrines, including holiness. They shared knowledge of some youths whose understanding was that holiness of life was not attainable in their lifetime, that some preachers mentioned holiness only "in passing" from the pulpit and not as a spiritual necessity. Now if the pulpit which is currently used by the majority of churches at least 50 times annually for the proclamation of biblical truth, which includes holiness, is in contrast to fourteen (14) annual bible Study sessions, there must be cause for concern. Not only is there the unattractiveness of such pulpit ministry, but there will be widespread carnality, the rule of self, rather than the sovereignty of the Holy Spirit in the church, and, by extension, this rule in the family and the society.

In summary, the holiness church must seize every opportunity to restructure its Christian education ministry, to regain the support of church families and community families in order to ensure that the lifestyle of holiness is experienced as our holiness heritage. The Sunday School ministry must be packaged, promoted and presented as the family Bible ministry; all annual Bible festivals must be used as an open opportunity to bring parents into this family

---

[52] Robert J. Choun & Michael S. Lawson, op. cit., p. 56

hour to observe what their children achieve from their training. Furthermore, the pastors must create opportunities to bond with the government schools in their communities to minister to the youth in particular according to the needs identified. In so doing, the church can achieve these goals through prayer, systematic planning and by spiritual tact and diplomacy for the good of the society and the glory of God.

We recognize and are grateful for the foundations laid by the missionaries under God for this thriving work through ninety years. To God be the glory. It is very clear that the wind of change is sweeping the world and the Caribbean area is no exception. The challenge to the Wesleyan Holiness Church is greater than ever. The prevailing drift of modern Christianity from biblical standards of doctrine and practice makes it incumbent upon the church to grasp and proclaim the holiness heritage. We must strive for the middle path of the highway of holiness in order to retain God's favour and power. By His grace, the Barbadian Wesleyan Holiness Church must not fail.

CHAPTER VII.
Holiness: The Development of Models for the Effective Communication of Holiness and Lifestyle Change for the Barbados Wesleyan Community

A. ANALYSIS OF CURRENT SYSTEMS

STRENGTHS OBSERVED

- There is a general awareness of the importance and the meaning of holiness.

- There is a unanimous desire to learn more about it and to see it demonstrated in the lifestyle of individuals.

- There is a consensus of agreement for a structured educational ministry, with the aim of effectively teaching doctrine generally and holiness in particular.

- There are about 10% of our pastors who have started to restructure their church teaching and discipleship programme with great membership appreciation.

- Some churches have been investing in the district's training for some of their members.

- One pastor stands ready to accept any structured assistance for the development of his church's teaching ministry.

- There is a strong appeal by the youth for individual talks on holiness through cell group discussions or zonal interaction among churches on the subject of holiness.

- There is a call for ongoing Christian education development for all leaders through training.

WEAKNESSES DISCOVERED

- A special need for local boards of administration to know their role in Christian education (i.e. recruiting and training policy, commitment to wholistic development of members).

- No job descriptions, no performance standards for staff evaluation.

- A weak vision plan, if any, for the teaching of core doctrines, including holiness, to the youth and new Christians by the majority of churches. Churches have registered an average of fourteen (14) Bible study sessions compared with an average of fifty (50) sermons annually.

- Some preachers only mention holiness in passing during their sermons.

- There is need for pastoral renewal in interest with respect to holiness.

OPPORTUNITIES TO BE SEIZED

- The environment for teaching is available.

- There is a cry for strategic planning, improved and relevant Bible study and Christian education development in the church.

- There is openness by some leaders for a new Christian education system in the local church.

- The youth have expressed a desire for teaching methods which would convince them that holiness is attainable by them in this lifetime.

- The Sunday School is a ripe harvest field for a structured programme for holiness indoctrination.

- New Christians need to be discipled in order to establish them in lifestyle holiness and involve them as teachers in doctrine for the future.

- Expository sermons must replace some of the vague topical sermons.

THREATS TO BE RECOGNISED AND WISELY HANDLED

- Pastors have got to evaluate the fact of carnality as a hindrance to spiritual growth and plot against it by teaching the Word of God and challenging each member to be filled with the Holy Spirit.

- Church leaders must recognize the loss of interest in members' response to the present teaching ministry and encourage feedback in order to apply corrective measures.

- Church leaders must avoid irrelevant methods of ministry which can impact negatively on church growth.

- Pastors need to be aware of negative body language of the congregation in response to their sermons and Bible study methods.

B. SUGGESTED RECOMMENDATIONS FOR TRANSMITTING OUR HERITAGE: CURRENT AND PROSPECTIVE EDUCATORS

This suggested programme is by no means static or exhaustive, it is hoped that it can be considered dynamic enough to be reviewed and revised periodically as the occasion demands. Judging by the present social climate of the land with the impact of technology and its accompanying forces on the life and lifestyles of its citizens, there will be need for a critical examination of adjusting the topics from time to time.

Current Leaders: Christian educators

Prospective Leaders: Church members between four (4) to six (6) years of Christian experience.

Aim of Course: To equip Christian educators and prospective church workers with the relevant doctrinal, leadership and communicative knowledge and skills for the enhancement of the Wesleyan holiness heritage.

Course Content:
(I) Sanctification: Initial, Entire and Progressive
(II) The Fullness of the Holy Spirit
(III) The Leadership of the Holy Spirit
(IV) Love: The Supreme Gift
(V) Leadership: Six Qualities of Effective Leadership; The Role and Challenges of Leadership

(VI) Communication

LESSON (I) SANCTIFICATION.

Initial, entire and, progressive sanctification are the work of the Holy Spirit within the life of man beginning, continuing and completing the miracle of holiness in the inner man.

This process begins at regeneration when man, as a practicing sinner, confesses and repents of his former sins. This stage is referred to as initial or partial, rather than entire, sanctification.

"We may say then that initial or partial Sanctification includes in its scope all that acquired pollution which attaches to the sinner's own acts; while entire Sanctification includes the cleansing from original sin or inherited depravity. Since sin is two-fold an act, and a state or condition, Sanctification must be two-fold… this gradual, preparatory work may be cut short in righteousness. When the sinner perfectly submits to the righteousness of Christ, and the spirit imparts new life to his soul. When, also, the child of God through the Spirit, fully renounces imbred sin and trusts the blood of cleansing, that moment he may, by simple faith in Christ, be sanctified wholly."[53]

Even as water baptism is instantaneous, and death is instantaneous, so is baptism with the Holy Spirit. Dying may be progressive, but death is a crisis — sudden, instantaneous. "Mortify [treat as dead] therefore your members which are upon the earth" (Colossians 3:5).

Progressive sanctification in no way nullifies instantaneous or entire sanctification. Rather, as one experiences the fullness of the Holy Spirit in His Lordship, he continues to fill one and cleanse one and empower one with His indwelling presence and power. "Be

---

[53] H. Orton Wiley, op. cit., pp. 481-482

filled with the Spirit" (Eph. 5:18) is the command to be continually soaked with the outpouring of the Holy Spirit.

LESSON (II) THE FULLNESS OF THE HOLY SPIRIT – EPH. 5:18; GAL. 5:22-25

(a) Definition: The complete control of one's life, one's ministry, one's total behaviour by the power of the Holy Spirit; the continuous empowerment of the Christian's life by the Holy Spirit.

(b) The Function of the Fullness of the Holy Spirit.

- Personal conquest over the mastery of the flesh. Gal. 5:16

  "…walk in the Spirit, and ye shall not fulfill the lust of the flesh."

- Personal victory over the daily practice of sin. Eph. 3:19

  "And to know the love of Christ, which passeth knowledge, that ye might be filled with all the fullness of God."

- Fruitfulness in Christian witness and service.

- Divine anointing in personal ministry. Eph. 5:18

  "…be filled with the Spirit."
- Divine companionship in daily living. Eph. 2:22

  "In whom you are also built together for a habitation of God through the Spirit."

LESSON (III) THE LEADERSHIP OF THE HOLY SPIRIT

The leadership of the Holy Spirit. St. John 16:13, 14

Definition: The authoritative guidance of the saint's life into God's destiny for his glory.

"The steps of a good man are ordered by the Lord ... and his seed is blessed." Psalm 37:23-26

SIX (6) WAYS IN WHICH THE HOLY SPIRIT PROVIDES LEADERSHIP

1. In Biblical ministry
2. In Life's vocation and business ventures (Acts 9:3; 13:1-3)
3. In Life's partnership and in decision making
4. In Holy living
5. In the discerning of satanic activities
6. In witnessing to the unsaved

LESSON (IV) LOVE: THE SUPREME GIFT
THE TEACHERS GUIDE

Love: The Supreme Gift – The Hallmark of Holiness
1 Corinthians 13

AIM: To enlighten Christian workers and prospective leaders to the quality of life the Holy Spirit provides for effecting change in any society.

Definition: Charity is that quality of love which alone is the gift of the Holy Spirit to the Spirit-filled saint for distinctive service.
A selfless concern for the welfare of even the most utterly unworthy.

The Christian faith is the only religious faith which is distinguished by love. This was Paul's declaration to the struggling Corinthian Church which was tainted by its pagan past, its multi-cultural challenges, and its carnal biases. Therefore, Paul seized the opportunity, as highlighted in I Corinthians 13, to present to this unstable church family the supremacy of love.

Paul, as he outlined to the Corinthians the several spiritual gifts, seemed to have been divinely diverted to present and define what is considered the most excellent quality of life: the fruit of the Holy Spirit.

I. THE SUPREMACY OF LOVE

A. Love is more than gifted speech. (v. 1)
As a tree is identified by its fruit, so is that person who is connected to the true vine – Jesus Christ. While spiritual gifts can be displayed by carnal Christians, love cannot be counterfeited. Love is more than gifted tongues or excellence of speech.

1. Love is the result of the purging of the human mind, the affection and the will by the blood of Jesus Christ. This is the result of purging of the human sinful nature and the subsequent formation of the divine nature within the consecrated Christian. Peter puts it beautifully in 2 Peter 1:3, 4 (NIV)...

"His divine power has given us everything we need for life and godliness through our knowledge of him who called us by his own glory and goodness. Through these he has given us his very great and precious promises, so that through them you may participate in the divine nature and escape the corruption in the world caused by evil desires."

2. Love is purity in all human relationships. Love is expressed by its nobility, its loyalty, its transparency of character.

3. Love is the authority for ministry. When love is absent from the lifestyle of the Christian, ministry will be severely weakened.

"I am only a resounding gong or a clanging cymbal…" 1 Cor. 13:1

"…if I have a faith that can move mountains, but have not love, I am nothing." 1 Cor. 13:2

Purity of life is power and passion for kingdom ministry. The fullness of the Holy Spirit is the only source of heart purity and authority for Christian ministry; purity and power must operate together!

B. Love is more valuable than gifted teaching and prophetic preaching.

1 Corinthians 13:2 (a) "If I have the gift of prophecy and can fathom all mysteries and all knowledge…but have not love, I am nothing."
Corinth was heavily influenced by various religious sects: their philosophies, their teachings, their devotion to their beliefs and subtlety of persuasion. However, Paul's message to the church was the necessity of the clear hallmark of

divine love. The eternal impact of Christian ministry must be anchored in love.

C. Love is more valuable than mountain-moving faith. 1 Cor. 13:2

D. Love is more beneficial than self-sacrifice. 1 Cor. 13:3

II. THE SIGNIFICANT CHARACTERISTICS OF LOVE

A. ITS DURABILITY (1 Cor. 13:4)

"Charity suffereth long and is kind…"

1. Love is slow to lose patience and is swift to find a way to be constructive.

2. Love is eternally trustworthy.

3. Love is spiritually blameless.

B. ITS PURITY

"Charity envieth not; charity vaunteth not itself, is not puffed up,"
1 Cor. 13:4 (b)

Love is spiritually sound in thought. It does not secretly wish for or grudge others for their achievements.

Love is socially reliable in its relationships. It is never celebrative at others' wrong doings. It is never graceless, rude nor insensitive to the feelings of others. Love is compassionate!

C. ITS CREDULITY – Its readiness to believe in, to trust even without evidence.

"Love believeth all things, hopeth all things," 1 Cor. 13:7

Love completely confides in and trusts:

1. In God – Jehovah.

    Love takes God seriously.

    Love takes God at His Word.

    Love is a covenant agreement.

2. In Brethren.

    Love is committed to believe the very best about the fellow brother and sister.

    Love is that attitude which never gives up on the fellow believer. It never leaves the wounded to die in isolation.

    "[A]nd over all these virtues put on love, which binds them all together in perfect unity." Col. 3:4

III. THE SUPREME EXPRESSION OF LOVE.

"Love never faileth:" 1 Cor. 13:8

Its commitment to unswerving intimacy:

1. The consistency of a personal commitment to its object.

2. The continuity of a personal loyalty to the source of love.

B. Its commitment to unending intimacy:

1. Life is incomplete without love.

2. Life is unfulfilled without love.

3. Life is unrealized without love: love is eternal.

LESSON (V) LEADERSHIP.
Teacher's Guide.

AIM: To empower eligible laymen to provide ongoing training for the local church's mission in transmitting the church's heritage and producing trusted leaders.

Definition of Leadership: The deliberate demonstration of influence to move people from where they are to a predetermined destination for their best interest.

"...The Lord said to Joshua son of Nun, Moses' aide: 'Moses my servant is dead. Now then, you and all these people, get ready to cross the Jordan River into the land I am about to give to them – to the Israelites.'" (Joshua 1:1, 2)

1. **SIX CRITICAL CHARACTERISTICS OF THE LEADER.**

    (a) Character

    (b) Vision

    (c) Courage

    (d) Influence

(e) A Good Listener

(f) A Great Thinker

2. THE ROLE OF THE LEADER.

"Only leaders can control (the) environment of their organization. They can be the change agents who create a climate conducive to growth."[54]

The leader must have the vision to reproduce other leaders by being:

1. A Model: The leader determines how the task ought to be done by personal demonstration. The trainee now has something at which to aim.

2. A Mentor: As leaders, it is alright to be seen and respected as big brothers; respect is earned. Trust will be reciprocated.

3. A Multipler: The leader's mission is to produce leaders who guarantee the continuation of a richer heritage.

Therefore, in order to produce better leaders, there must be the investing in and the sowing of leaders.

3. SOME CHALLENGES OF LEADERSHIP

To be assured of God's call to a specific leadership task.

Commitment to continual leadership development.

The purpose to grow to one's full potential.

To produce better leaders than oneself.

---

[54] John C. Maxwell, <u>Developing Leaders Around You</u>, (Tennessee: Nelson Publishers, 1995), pp. 19, 20

To maintain the Holy Spirit's anointing on one's life and leadership.

To be a good listener.

LESSON VI COMMUNICATION
Teacher's Guide

AIM: To assist church public speakers in the art of transferring information in a manner that can be understood with great satisfaction.

DEFINITION: The transmitting of a message from one subject, person or creature to another, so that both subjects understand the message with the desired effect.

The transfer of information, from one subject to another, in a common language to ensure reception and understanding.

1. COMMUNICATION MEDIA AND METHODS.

The forms of communication generally fall into two main groups: verbal and nonverbal. Inasmuch as each person is special and the world is now one village, cultural differences are important as well.

"Human communication occurs through the use of one or more of twelve different signal systems.

"The twelve signal systems are the spoken word, written word, audio, numerical, kinetic, pictorial, artifactual, touch, space, time, smell and optical.

"The loud signals (spoken, written, audio) often dominate the remaining silent signals which in turn greatly affect our credibility."[55]

2. COMMUNICATION REQUIRES THE FOLLOWING FIVE KEY ELEMENTS

A Communicator — a person or persons with a message to be sent to others with a specific purpose.

A message — that information which is desired to be relayed in the selected or common signal system or language.

The medium — the selected form or channel to process the message: face to face by verbal interaction, written correspondence or mass media.

Audience — the person or group who is the target of the message.

Feedback — the response from the target group indicating understanding and appreciation or restlessness, rejection and disappointment.

3. RELEVANT CAUTIONS IN COMMUNICATION

Be very sensitive and understanding in relation to your audience.

Let your language be appropriate to the occasion and audience (dialect, etc.): standard English.

Be sincere in your speech and your body language: Be Christian!

---

[55] James F. Engel, <u>Getting Your Message Across</u>, (Philippines: OMF Literature INC. 1989), p. 114

Do not talk "down" to your audience; please respect your audience.

Let your audience know, by telling them, that they are special and let it be seen!

4. THE SIGNIFICANCE OF LISTENING TO EFFECTIVE COMMUNICATION

Many speakers are prone to get their message across to their audience at the expense of paying close attention to what the audience is saying by their feedback.

A. SOME BENEFITS OF A GOOD LISTENING ATTITUDE

It enhances interpersonal relationships.

It provides helpful information from the audience about the message and messenger.

It is a reliable medium by which the communicator can improve his performance and attitude toward criticism and compliments.

It enhances the audience's good opinion of itself.

It develops a "win/win" attitude.

B. SOME SUGGESTIONS FOR IMPROVING ONE'S LISTENING SKILLS

Listen to the complete message before you interpret or respond.

Listen to the verbal as well as the non-verbal components of the speakers: gestures, tone of voice and facial expressions.

Listen for ideas not just to the words.

Avoid distractions and interruptions of all kinds.

Be positive and kind without inserting any personal biases.

Repeat the message to the messenger to be sure that what you heard and understood was indeed what was intended.

5. SOME BARRIERS TO EFFECTIVE COMMUNICATION

Being unprepared for the occasion: insufficient data.

Emotional imbalance and lack of confidence.

Limited command of the language.

Different speech accent.

Lack of trust between messenger and audience.

Feedback during presentation.

Inadequate preparation of the physical facilities: the sound system, the lighting and air-conditioning.

The attitude of snobbery and self-centredness.

SUMMARY

Man is not an island unto himself, rather, he is a social and spiritual being in particular. Therefore, he has needs which he cannot satisfy on his own. People need people. Progress is possible only through effective communication; without it there would be: family disintegration, great social decay, political collapse and obvious human destruction.

Conversely, effective communication is life and hope to mankind and his society. So, be reminded that, "Communication is the means by which we transfer truth. Communication can move and mould men, individually and collectively. Communication lays the very foundation for spiritual decisions. It relates intimately to a person's relationship with God. If effective communication is so important, does it not follow that leaders, redeemed and called of God, ought to give sober attention to the most effective way of utilizing this powerful tool?..."[56]

SUGGESTED NEW LIFE COURSE FOR BEGINNER CHRISTIANS, SCHOOL STUDENTS AND YOUTH

LESSON I: THE NEW LIFE

AIM: To provide scriptural and spiritual nourishment for healthy growth for babes three months to three years in Christ.

METHOD: Discussion with lively interaction.

OUTLINE

I. THE DEFINITION OF THE 'NEW LIFE' AND SOME SCRIPTURAL REFERENCES.

  A. The communication of spiritual life by the Holy Spirit to a soul dead in sin. Eph. 2:1-2

  B. The deliverance of the sinner from the practice of sin. Eph. 2:4-6

  C. To be born-again. St. John 3:3-6

---

[56] John Haggai, Lead On, (Texas: Word Book Publisher, 1986), p. 89

D. The miraculous transformation of desires and affections. 2 Cor. 5:17

II. OTHER RELATED TERMS USED FOR THE 'NEW LIFE'

A. Redemption and Regeneration.

1. The quickening of the soul from the bondage of sin. Eph. 2:1

2. The passing from spiritual death to life in Christ. St. John 5:24

B. Justification by faith.

That judicial act of God pronouncing those who believe in and accept the sacrifice of Jesus' life at Calvary are set free from the guilt of sin through faith in Jesus Christ.

THE SUMMARY OF NEW LIFE

The new life or conversion is the principal result of the atoning grace of Jesus Christ. This great gift from God is possible only through the miracle of salvation. Man is not only brought into right relationship with God, but man's attitude toward sin is also changed.

LESSON II THE NEW LIFE (CONTINUED)

Some clear evidences of the new life.

INTRODUCTION　　When one repents of personal sins and accepts Jesus Christ as Lord of one's life, at that very moment one is forgiven of all former "sins" and is immediately accepted into the family of God.

SOME EVIDENCES OF NEW LIFE

A. The witness of the Holy Spirit. Romans 8:15,16; 1 John 5:10; Galatians 4:6

The inner assurance of personal acceptance with God is impressed upon one's conscience by the Holy Spirit. The Holy Spirit, the third "Person" of the Holy Trinity, is the person who convicts the sinner of sin and assures him of redemption upon personal confession of sin.

B. The witness of the Human Spirit.

The penitant person, upon his confession of sin, not only receives the witness of the Holy Spirit of sins forgiven, but he also experiences inner peace.

C. Victory over the sinful past. 1 John 2:29; 3:9.

D. Personal faith. 1 John 5:4

E. Changed attitude toward God and godliness.

LESSON III STRUCTURAL DEVELOPMENT FOR NEW CONVERTS.

AIM: To challenge the new Christians to relate confidently to God and the brethren, and to begin sharing their new experience with others.

ENGAGEMENT IN

A. PRAYER

Prayer is conversing with God either privately or corporately: communion with God through adoration or praise, petition or intercession, personal confession of failure and thanksgiving in Jesus name. St. Matthew 6:9-18; St. Luke 4:1-21

B. BIBLE READING

New Christians ought to read the Word for: acquaintance, clarification, understanding and guidance for effective living. Discuss each component for understanding, and practice Bible reading in the class for 30 minutes.

The first three months – personal schedule for Bible Reading: Psalms 1-50; Proverbs 1-25; St. John 1-15; Colossians 1-3.

C. CORPORATE WORSHIP

Hebrews 10:23-25; Acts 2:41-47; Acts 4:23-33.

What is corporate worship? Discuss.

D. DISCIPLESHIP MINISTRY BY PASTOR AND REPRESENTATIVE

METHODS OF SHARING ONE'S FAITH IN JESUS

1. Preparation for water baptism.

   A. The significance of water baptism: the physical declaration of one's death to the past life of sin.

   B. Example of candidates for water baptism.

      - Jesus Christ. St. Matthew 3:11-17; St. Mark 1:9

      - Converts at Samaria. Acts 8:12-39

- The Ethopian Eunuch. Acts 8:27

- Saul of Tarsus. Acts 9: 18

1. Preparation for church membership and all personal rites: teach the basic doctrine of the church from the Wesleyan Holiness Discipline 2003.

2. Teach a simple method of sharing Jesus Christ using St. John 3:16.

    - You are special. Jesus died for you.

    - You are disconnected from God; you are a practicing sinner.

    - You can be forgiven NOW, if you only repent of your sin.

LESSONS IV & V DOCTRINAL DEVELOPMENT FOR THE NEW BELIEVER

AIM: To expose the new believer to the systematic indoctrination of the Word of God.

1. The definition of sin.

    A. Sin and its consequences. Genesis 2:15-17

    Man's innocence. Genesis 2:15-17

    Man's temptation. Genesis 3:1-5

    Man's disobedience. Genesis 3:6-10

Man's sin and judgment. Genesis 3:14-24; Romans 3:23

B. Sin and its remedy. Genesis 3:15

The woman and her seed. Genesis 3:15

The serpent and his defeat. Genesis 3:15; Isaiah 9:6, 7; Isaiah 53

The human family and our victory. Romans 5:12; 6:23; Romans 10:9-11; 16:20

2. THE DOCTRINE OF THE TRINITY – THE SOVEREIGN CREATOR, RULER, REDEEMER.

"We believe in the one living and true God, both holy and loving, eternal, unlimited in power, wisdom and goodness, the creator and preserver of all things. Within this unity there are three persons of one essential nature, power, and eternity – the Father, the Son and the Holy Spirit."[57]

Gen. 1:1; Exodus 6:4; Isaiah 40:28, 29; St. Matthew 3:16,17; 28:19; St. John 1:1-2; 4:24; Col. 1:16, 17

THE FATHER

"We believe the Father is the source of all that exists, whether of matter or spirit. With the Son and the Holy Spirit, He made man in His image. By intention He relates to man as Father, thereby forever declaring His goodwill toward man in love, He both seeks and receives penitant sinners."[58]

Isaiah 64:8; St. Matthew 7:11; St. John 3:17; Romans 8:15.

---

[57] The Wesleyan Holiness Discipline 2003, (Indiana: Wesley Press), p. 32
[58] Ibid., P.33

Rev. Dr. Carlyle Williams

THE SON OF GOD

His Incarnation. St. John 1:1-18; Phil. 2:5-11

His Crucifixion – Atonement for sin.

His Resurrection.

His Ascension.

His Return and Rapture of the church.

Scriptural references: St. John 1:1-18; 3:1-29; 1 Cor. 15; Isaiah 52:13-15; 53:1-12;Col. 1:15-20; Hebrews 9:11-15; 24-28; Revelation 19:11-16; 20:6-20

THE HOLY SPIRIT

I. The Promise of the Holy Spirit's coming.

II. The Person and Presence of the Holy Spirit.

III. The Power of the Holy Spirit.

"We believe in the Holy Spirit who proceeds from the Father and the Son, and is of the same essential nature, majesty and glory as the Father and the Son, truly and eternally God. He is the Administrator of grace to all mankind, and is particularly the effective Agent in conviction for sin, in regeneration in Sanctification and in glorification. He is ever present, assuring, preserving, guiding, and enabling the believer."[59] St. John 14, 15, 16; St. Luke 24:49; Acts 1-5

---

[59] Ibid., P.34

LESSON VI FIVE STEPS TO A WEEKLY SPIRITUAL GROWTH PROGRAMME

AIM: To empower the new believer to be responsible for his daily private spiritual nutrition and to be accountable to his teacher once a week.

Personal devotions are recommended on a daily basis, preferably early each day. However, in addition to your daily devotions, here is an outline of a weekly spiritual growth programme for a complete year.

Monday	One hour with God and your Bible.
Tuesday	One hour listening to a tape of your pastor's sermon.
Wednesday	Another hour with the same tape (including time filing notes on highlights and reflecting on what has been learned.)
Thursday	One hour reading a recommended spiritual book.
Friday	Another hour with the same book filing notes and meditating on what has been learned.

QUESTIONS

Is God speaking to me through my Bible study?

Are you consciously communicating with God in prayer?

What changes have you observed in your new life?

Rev. Dr. Carlyle Williams

THE PURPOSES OF THE DEVELOPMENT OF MODELS

1. THE EFFECTIVE ENLIGHTENING OF CHURCH MEMBERS AND NONCHURCH MEMBERS

There is an urgent need by the church for the redefining of the premier doctrine of the Wesleyan Church. This doctrine is not a status symbol but, on the contrary, it is a declaration of a divine requirement for effective Christian living and ministering in every generation. Furthermore, it is the divine entrance requirement to heaven.

This writer has discovered through his survey a very strong call for an effective teaching ministry on the doctrine of holiness in particular and other basic biblical doctrines in general. Knowledge produces confidence, competence and authority.

Therefore, given the difficulties of weak educational programmes in the current church ministry, it was worthwhile to produce sample curricula for the way forward. These are recommended for selected Christian educators as well as for all children, youth and members who have been in the church up to six years, thus ensuring the kind of education for the establishing of a solid foundation upon which the local church needs to build for the enlighting of a ready community.

The youth are requesting a structured educational ministry in the Sunday School department and the youth department. New converts are very dissatisfied with the level of discipling to which they are generally exposed. Furthermore, in many cases, the teaching is the lecture method without very much interaction and unchallenging at best.

2. THE DELIBERATE EMPOWERING OF CHURCH MEMBERS FOR POWER BASED MINISTRIES

Spiritual ministry demands spiritual energy and divine authority because the Christian has to engage a subtle spiritual enemy every moment of every day. It is God's purpose to put the spiritual resources at the disposal of every Christian who is prepared to make the necessary commitment.

The military spends billons of dollars in the preparation of its forces to be on the leading edge of warfare. Those recruits must be exposed to the discipline of long and consistent hours of training to build endurance, skills and the necessary knowledge to take out the enemy, whoever it may be.

The Christian church must understand that it is similarly expected to develop the necessary structures to make and keep its soldiers battle-fit and ready to win in the fight against sin. Then we must train! Train and train! Christian educators must be selected with the understanding of what is expected of them in relation to their commitment to duty, concern for the lives of their students and their accountability to God for their stewardship.

The models presented in this research paper are not only for information but also for the stimulating of creativity, the triggering of the latent skills within the student teachers in discovering and developing their gifts for service. It is a known fact that many church workers are insecure because they are not encouraged to exploit their potential. Human beings are like rubber bands which are most effective only when they are stretched.

3. THE ULTIMATE GOAL OF EVANGELIZING OUR COMMUNITIES THROUGH THE WESLEYAN CHURCHES

The church is on a mission: discipling the flock and multiplying the fold through evangelism. Jesus spent three years teaching and modeling His message and ministry as he engaged His twelve disciples. Jesus left His scrip enshrined in the Holy Word. Therein are the messages of redemption, the methods of follow-up and the ministry of the Holy Spirit to achieve spiritual goals of Kingdom building.

The Wesleyan Church must always be aware of its divine mission and be taught how to effect that mission through information. This study would have been incomplete without the presentation of sample lessons of those vital subjects for the equipping of teachers, students, new believers and even the unconverted in our commitment to inflict substantial damage upon the kingdom of darkness. Let us trim the lamps of education and let them burn with knowledge in this time of moral and spiritual disarray. Darkness will never put out light; let us then enlighten, edify and empower the church through the leadership of the Holy Spirit.

CONCLUSION

The time is ripe for each Local Board of Administration to redefine its purpose in relation to church development and the role of the Christian education, as it relates to the total church vision and mission for this generation. The educational and spiritual ministry goals of a church must be based on the needs of its children and converts as well as the church's philosophy of teaching sound doctrine and seeing the demonstration of the same in lifestyle ministry.

RECOMMENDATIONS

It is very clear from my investigations that there is major concern about Christian education personnel and their effectiveness. The thinking suggests the need for proper recruitment, training and retention plans for teaching staffs. Some of the needs in this area are:

1. PERSONNEL GOALS

- Long-term commitment to build teacher-student environment.

- Pre-service and in-service training on a continuing basis.

- Continual recruitment of staff prior to need of them.

- Clearly defined job descriptions.

- Required regular staff meetings for planning, problem solving, mentoring, praying and training.

- Required staff attendance at all meetings.

- Required commitment to personal development.

2. EDUCATIONAL GOALS

- Unified curricula for all age groups, to ensure coverage of Bible subjects, continuity of teaching and learning styles, and coordination of programmes.

- Established policies and procedures that are clearly communicated to parents, staff and students.

- A balance of worship, instruction, expression and fellowship.

- Bible memorization and homework.

- Evangelism and visitation.

- Discipleship as an ongoing passion and policy of the local board of administration.

- Recording of students' progress and the systematic evaluation of curricula and staff.

3. SPIRITUAL GOALS

- Teach for spiritual responses.

- Provide for maturity in Christ.

- Aim at holistic development. St. Luke 2:52

    - Develop tough thinkers.

    - Encourage ready helpers.

    - Insist on and demonstrate punctuality.

    - Award excellence.

- Follow-up on all spiritual decisions: bew birth, entire sanctification, the call to Christian service, etc.

- Lead children to church membership and ministry involvement.

The church has to work directly with its community. Some churches and pastors affirm their responsibility to contribute to the spiritual development of members but often fail to back up that affirmation with time, money and planning. The pastor must spend quality time in prayer, planning and presenting relevant and innovative programmes with the view of leading his flock to maturity in faith and in ministry.

Children's ministry: Sunday School, junior church or children's meetings provide the structural framework, not only for the church of tomorrow, but also for the corporate society of today: the leaders in the home, the staff of our day schools, the professionals for the Caribbean Single Market and Economy (C.S.M.E) the decision makers in parliament and church leaders.

Let us therefore, read the times; let us respond to the times and let us redirect the times. "And the Word of God increased; and the number of the disciples multiplied in Jerusalem greatly; and a great company of the priests were obedient to the faith" (Acts 6:7). This faith includes the faith of our fathers, that body of truth that was once delivered to the saints which has now become our heritage. Let us be diligent as the church of today to employ every God-given media as the means to urgently transmit the tradition of holiness as a Wesleyan heritage to our succeeding generations, because there can be no true and lasting success without a successor. Let us then aspire together, and let us achieve together in the power of the Holy Spirit.

I have been enlightened, enriched and empowered, and my desire is to share the benefits of this book with the view of initiating holistic change in this wonderful Wesleyan Holiness family church.

Rev. Dr. Carlyle Williams

I sincerely hope that our efforts as a denomination will be to make a fervent plea and impact for us as God's people to continue in special supplication and action, to request God's direction and special anointing on our specific concern, and to transmit our heritage and tradition to our youth and general congregation.

BIBLIOGRAPHY

Barnhart, Clarence L.

Barnhart, Robert K., The World Book Dictionary. Chicago: World Book INC. 1963

Bend, J., Historical Development of the Wesleyan Church Barbados

Benson, Clarence H., Sunday School Success. Indiana: Wesley Press, 1978

Brubaker J. Omar and Robert E. Clarke, Understanding People. Indiana: Wesley Press, 1977

Choun, Robert and Michael S. Lawson, The Christian Educators Handbook on Children's Ministry. Michigan: Baker Book House Co., 1998

Duewel, Wesley L., Ablaze For God. Michigan: Zondervan Publishing House, 1989

Ives, R. Wingrov, A Missionary Cry From The Island of Barbados. Kentucky: Missionary Office, 1930

Jessop, Harry E., Foundations of Doctrine. Indiana: The Free Methodist Publishing House, 1946

Kendall, R.T., The Anointing: Yesterday, Today, Tomorrow. Florida: Charisma House, 2003

Lawrence, Marion, My Message To Sunday School Workers. New York: Harper and Brothers Publishers, 1924

Maxwell, John C., Developing the Leaders Around You. Tennessee: Nelson Publishers, 1995

Maxwell, John C., The 21 Indispensable Qualities of A Leader. Tennessee: Nelson Publishers, 1999

Prior, Kenneth, The Way of Holiness. Great Britain: Christian Freus Publications Ltd, 1982

Purkiser, W.T., Exploring Our Faith. Missouri: Beacon Hill Press, 1966

Philip, H.A., Minutes of The Ninth Annual Assembly of The Pilgrim Holiness Church Barbados. Advocate Press, 1940

Smithen, Vernon. C.W.C 50TH Anniversary Souvenir Journal. Barbados, 1992

Sanders, J. Oswald. Spiritual Leadership. Chicago: Moody Press, 1994

Taylor, Richard S., Life In The Spirit. Missouri: Beacon Hill Press, 1966

Wilcox, Leslie D. Be Ye Holy. Ohio: The Revivalist Press, 1965

Wiley, H. Orton, Christian Theology Vol. II. Missouri: Beacon Hill Press, 1966

The Discipline of The Wesleyan Holiness Church 2003. Indiana: Wesley Press, 2003

Preacher's Magazine. Missouri: Beacon Hill Press, 1986

Wilkenson, Bruce. 30 Days To Discovering Personal Victory Through Holiness. U.S.A.: Multnomah Publishers INC., 2003

Wilson, Earl L., Pastoral Letter. Indiana: Wesley Press, 1996

TESTIMONIALS

The book, *Repositioning Our Church through Our Holiness Heritage*, reflects the many years of serious reflection on the cardinal and foundational teaching of the Wesleyan Holiness Church. Not only are the doctrinal issues highlighted, but careful historical data and New Life Courses for the improvement of spiritual life are provided. Thoughtful readers will be seriously challenged to dispute the hypothesis of the author when he states that the church must return to its holiness heritage.

Dr. Nigel L. Taylor
President, Barbados Evangelical Association

"The content is very easily understood while being theologically sound. Being a student of theology, I found many books on the same issue that were bogged down by a myriad of theological terms, making assimilation of the information rather difficult."

I believe very strongly that this book is going to serve as a catalyst to jump start a holiness-thinking and quest in those in the holiness church environment.

We thank God for the Rev. Carlisle Williams!

Dr. Scoffield Eversley
President,
Caribbean Nazarene College
Republic of Trinidad & Tobago

This book not only saves the history of the Wesleyan Church in Barbados, but it will also continue to be a guide to disciples seeking full devotion to their Master. What He calls us to be, He provides the grace to become. We clearly are called unto holiness by a holy God. 1 Peter 1: 15-16, "But just as he who called you is holy, so be holy in all you do; for it is written: 'Be holy, because I am holy.'" Certainly He will do His part to make us become exactly that. This is the message of biblical holiness that is summarized in this book.

Rev. Shelton Wood, Jr., PhD, EdD, DMin
President, Georgetown Wesleyan University (www.GWUA.net)

About the Author

The Rev. Dr. Carlyle Williams currently serves as the District Superintendent of the Wesleyan Holiness Church in the island of Barbados in the Caribbean. He has held this office for the past Twenty-one (21) years. He has also served the Caribbean General Church as General Secretary of Evangelism and Missions for four (4) years.

Rev. Dr. Carlyle Williams is a graduate of Caribbean Wesleyan College with a Diploma in Christian Theology; Guyana Wesleyan College with a Masters Degree in Christian Ministry; Georgetown Wesleyan University of the Americas with a Doctorate in Christian Leadership and Ministry and Haggai Institute in Singapore in Advanced Leadership Skills. His Thirty-Eight (38) years in ministry has contributed greatly to the development of the Caribbean Church community and beyond.